THE MIDDLE SCHOOL — HIGH ROAD OR DEAD END?

Woburn Educational Series
General Editor:
Peter Gordon, Institute of Education, University of London

The Middle School—

High Road
or Dead End?

John Burrows

THE WOBURN PRESS

First published 1978 in Great Britain by
THE WOBURN PRESS
Gainsborough House, Gainsborough Road,
London E11 1RS, England

and in the United States of America by
THE WOBURN PRESS
c/o Biblio Distribution Centre
81 Adams Drive, P.O. Box 327, Totowa, N.J. 07511

Copyright © 1978 John Burrows

ISBN 0 7130 0149 6

Printed in Great Britain by The Bourne Press, Bournemouth

Contents

Illustrations between pp. 24–25, 40–41, 184–185, 200–201

Foreword

This book requires a word of explanation, since its purpose differs somewhat from that of other recent publications on middle schools. It is written in response to requests from parents, school managers, students (often those not specialising in this field), and professional colleagues and visitors from other countries—people who take an informed interest in English education but who do not necessarily need either statistical or technical detail. Many teachers too have expressed a wish for a study of this kind. The kind of question which I have tried to answer is searching yet not suited to cut-and-dried replies. Are middle schools good or bad? How did they happen? What is distinctive about them? Do they increase educational opportunity or restrict it? And, if they are good, why do they crop up here but not there?

Such questions cannot be fairly answered in a vacuum. They call for at least an outline statement of the social, political and educational context in which middle schools arose, of the structure of local and national government so far as it affects them, of the role and resources of teachers, administrators, advisers, architects and others, and of the performance of typical middle schools to date. I ask the indulgence of English readers who find some of the ground all too familiar (the historical sketch in Chapter 1 in particular is intended to help those not familiar with the intricacies of the English system and its origins); my experience is nevertheless that even the informed observer is sometimes grateful for a new angle on what he knows.

It has been my good fortune to have had close touch since the early 1960s with middle schools and with many of those who, almost literally, thought them into being. The experience has been by turns exhilarating, encouraging, frustrating and exasperating; but that the middle school has become a powerhouse of educational potential, I have no doubt. The judgements made in this book draw widely upon the experience and convictions of those working in and for middle schools; where they are my own alone, I believe they are built on solid fact.

No acknowledgements could do justice to the kindness and understanding of so many who have helped me—the heads and staffs of middle schools in many parts of the country, education officers and advisers, members of the staffs of university departments and colleges of education, and my former colleagues in H.M. Inspectorate and the Architects and Buildings Branch of the Department of Education and Science. Special thanks are due to Mr. S. F. H. Johnson and Mr. J. Jervis, of Ridgeway Middle School, Redditch, to Mr. J. D. Rees of Elmgrove Middle School, Harrow, and to Mr. K. J. Werrett of Westacre Middle School, Droitwich, all of whom have kindly made photographs and illustrations available. It is a particular pleasure to record my thanks to two pupils of Ridgeway Middle School, Nicholas Havas and Justin Jones, who not only gave up free time in order expertly to process a large number of photographs (only a few of which, owing to considerations of space, can be included), but in so doing demonstrated most effectively the range and quality of skills which could be acquired in their own school. I am grateful also to the Controller of H.M. Stationery Office for permission to reproduce design plans from Building Bulletin No. 35, to Berrow's Newspapers Ltd., of Worcester, for the photograph on page 000 and to the Education Authorities of Bradford, Buckinghamshire and Hampshire for help with some of the design plans.

July 1977   J.B.

PART 1

THE FRAMEWORK

CHAPTER 1

The Long March of History

'Only after the working classes of the towns had been enfranchised by the Reform Act of 1867 did the politicians say: *We must educate our masters*'.

(G. M. Trevelyan: *English Social History*)

What are these *middle schools* they keep talking of? . . .
The children are to stay an extra year in the village school?
But what'll they do? . . .
But surely they'll be worse off? I mean, look at the things the Grammar School's got, the labs, the gym, the music rooms . . .
And what about the examination courses? . . .
Who decided all this? Have we got to put up with it?

This batch of questions from some typical parents on being told of the changes which were in prospect for their local schools gives voice to two of the main anxieties inseparable from educational change; the fear that the new and untried will work to the disadvantage of their own children (and there is a widespread and healthy dislike among British parents of having their children treated as guinea-pigs, as many of them express it), and bewilderment about how such changes happen. Who decides, and why?

The middle school is a new institution. Such fears are natural, and there is always an element of risk in change; yet change there must be, or society stagnates. Is the middle school a sign of new, dynamic educational thinking, a trail-blazer which will enliven English education; is it an unjustified piece of tinkering with the system for purposes, as some opponents of secondary re-organisation have put it, of social engineering; or is it, in the phrase of one educationist, just a gimmick which is irrelevant to the main purposes of education? And who is responsible for its introduction, and why is it not universal, but springing up just here and there? To give answers to questions such as these it is necessary to take a brief look at the structure of education in the United Kingdom and in particular at the division of responsibilities within it. This can only be done historically, for it is events rather than theories which have moulded the system into what it is today.

Our concern is with England and Wales. There is a measure of regionalism in the conduct of many public services in the United Kingdom, and education is one. Though Acts of Parliament passed by the United Kingdom Parliament at Westminster and given the assent of the monarch apply to the whole of the United Kingdom unless parts of it are specifically excluded, education in Scotland and in Northern Ireland is actually administered there under regional arrangements and, within the lines of policy laid down in the Acts, there is a good deal of local variation. The Secretary of State for Education and Science at Westminster is responsible for the service in England and Wales only; education in Scotland is the responsibility of his Cabinet colleague, the Secretary of State for Scotland. (Arrangements for Northern Ireland are at present of an interim character, but are the responsibility of the Minister for Northern Ireland.) Our consideration of the middle school is confined to England, however, for the sole but convincing reason that in Scotland, Wales and Northern Ireland no education authority has introduced middle schools or plans to do so. The middle school in the United Kingdom is so far a purely English phenomenon.

How the System Evolved

The history of the national system of education has not been one of placid development. It had to be fought for, and the lines of its development were often keenly, even bitterly, contested. Government involvement dates back less than one hundred and fifty years, and in the first half of that period, as the quotation from Professor Trevelyan heading this chapter indicates, it was a reluctant involvement so far as most politicians were concerned; progress was due to the dedicated efforts of the few. These few however were responding to a deep-rooted desire for education on the part of the new and rapidly increasing populations of the industrial towns; the tide was flowing with them and, by the turn of the century, both major political parties, Liberals and Conservatives, had accepted a free, universal system of schooling, with growing opportunities for higher education arising from it, as a necessary and natural responsibility of the State.

Between 1700 and 1800 the population of the country nearly doubled, from five and a half to nine million; in the first half of the nineteenth century it doubled again. But in the industrial towns the rate of growth was faster still—in Leeds, for instance, the population rose from 53,000 to 172,000 between 1801 and 1851, in Sheffield from 46,000 to 135,000, in Manchester and Salford from 90,000 to 400,000. The earliest attempt at an educational census, and one clearly subject to a substantial margin of error, was made by Lord Kerry in 1833 and showed the astonishing figure of one person in eleven of the entire population of England and Wales attending day-schools of some kind. Clearly the people wanted education.

The schools available to them were of three kinds. Around half were 'self-supporting', i.e. privately owned, and they must have included a wide range of the good and wholesome, the squalid and bad. Second, some fortunate areas had schools endowed by benefactors for the education of local children; some of these dated back to the time of the first Queen Elizabeth or even earlier, and many were known as grammar schools, a term which has continued in use until the present day and which originally denoted studies based on language, literature and religion. Third, and most important, were the 'public subscription' schools, run by trusts or societies set up and supported by the well-to-do in an often heroic attempt to meet the seemingly insatiable demand of the working classes for basic education.

Two societies in particular were large and, in the educational debates of the next half-century, influential; they were also often in bitter rivalry. The British and Foreign Schools Society, set up by Joseph Lancaster, a Quaker, drew strong support from the Nonconformist denominations ('the sects', as their opponents slightingly designated them). Alongside it was the National Society (its full title was the 'National Society for Promoting the Education of the Poor in the Principles of the Established Church') founded by Dr. Andrew Bell, a Church of England clergyman, and harnessing the charitable and educational impulses of that church.

The schools of both societies were run on the so-called monitorial principle, a type of organisation evolved separately by both Lancaster and Bell; it consisted, briefly, of the master teaching the lessons for the day in advance to some of the older pupils, who in their turn each taught them to a small group of pupils, parrot fashion. Mass tests and, in some of the larger schools, even a system of communication by manual signalling between master and monitors, ensured that the pupils had the lessons off by heart. The great advantage of the method was that through it a small number of teachers could instruct a very large number of children, a vital matter for societies of limited financial resources; and it was not until the 1850s that the reports of HM Inspectors showed plainly that, though the pupils might memorise much by this method, little was effectively understood.

It was beyond the power of voluntary effort to meet the needs. Continued pressure and humanitarian benevolence eventually dragged a reluctant Government into some kind of formal participation in education, oddly enough through the medium of the Factory Act of 1833, which included provisions for the compulsory education for two hours daily of children working in factories. Since no source of funds was designated for the purpose, this section of the Act rapidly became a dead letter. The same impulses however also moved the Government, more practically, to make a grant for the purpose of building schools to the two main agencies actually at work, the National Society and the British and Foreign Schools Society. The initial grant in 1833 was £20,000, equally divided between the two; and, however thin was the wedge, it established the precedent that the central Government should assume some measure of responsibility for the education of the nation's children and that one method of discharging it was through partnership with voluntary bodies. Though much changed in degree, these two principles were generally accepted and they continue in the educational system to this day.

Not without challenge, admittedly. Especially in Parliament, education in the 1830s was an inflammatory topic. The Church of England was determined that popular education should include instruction in its own doctrines; but other denominations were equally determined that no such monopoly in the salvation of souls should be permitted. In 1839 a Government proposal to set up its own training college for teachers (very much needed) was so fiercely contested in the House of Commons, because it appeared to loyal Anglicans to weaken the role of the Church of England, that the annual grant was approved only by the tightrope margin of 275 votes to 273, and in the Lords the Government actually suffered the indignity of a vote of censure. This, however, was the worst moment. In the same year a Committee of the Privy Council was set up to exercise oversight of the distribution and use of the Government grants to the societies. Its staff included a Secretary and two inspectors, who had right of entry to the schools of the benefiting societies and whose task was to report on the education given and the value, in effect, which the country was getting for its money.

The first Secretary, James Kay (later Sir James Kay Shuttle-worth), was a man of independent mind and enlightened ideas, and it was largely his humanising influence and the steady, patient work of the inspectors under his command that led, in the next twenty-five years, to a better understanding of the real nature of education and of the benefits which could accrue to the nation from it. Concern over illiteracy and over the uneven spread of schools grew steadily, so that ensuing legislation did not have to undergo the fierce ordeals of the 1830s. The country's mood was such that the Electoral Reform Act of 1867 could

hardly fail to lead to the great Education Act of 1870, the
guarantee that education should become the right of, and the
requirement of, every child in the land.

The Bi-partisan Years

It had taken nearly forty years for central government to accept
the full implications of what it had done in 1833; but, once
begun, there was no turning back on the road leading to universal, free, compulsory schooling. It was moreover a road which
both major political parties came to tread, so that changes of
government delayed the process very little. The great leap
forward was taken by W. E. Gladstone's Liberal Government
in the Education Act of 1870, piloted by W. E. Forster, a
Bradford industrialist who was convinced of the social and
economic benefits of an educated workforce. This Act re-
asserted the need for partnership between State and voluntary
agencies by doubling the grant to the existing societies and by
placing Roman Catholic schools on the same footing; but in
addition it laid upon the State the entirely new obligation of
setting up its own schools in those places where there were no
voluntary schools undertaking the educational task.

The Government had however no intention of building and
running these new schools itself; the principle of agency held
good. This time the agencies were to be local School Boards,
drawing most of their funds from central government sources
but being empowered to raise a proportion from ratepayers
locally. Thus was established the principle that State education
is essentially a locally provided service, complying with overall
government policies and drawing from central government the
larger part of its funds, but within these limits able to meet local
needs and preferences as locally seems best.

There are numerous major legislative landmarks since 1870,
but they extend, rather than change, this basic structure. In
1876 a Conservative government tightened the obligations on
parents to send their children to school; in 1880 a Liberal
Government made it compulsory, and in 1891 a Conservative

administration decreed that the Board schools should be run without direct cost to parents. Thus far, the State had limited its own provision to the first stages, or *elementary* education; but in 1902 another legislative landmark imposed upon county councils and county borough councils the duty of providing *secondary* education also. These large councils replaced the much smaller School Boards as the 'local education authorities' (LEAs), and it is from this time that the use of this familiar term dates. From 1902 until 1944 the State-provided elementary schools were popularly known as 'council schools'. These local education authorities were instructed to work in partnership with, not to compete against, voluntary schools already at work in the area. This partnership of county (i.e. LEA) schools working alongside voluntary schools, has continued amicably, though during this present century the cost of meeting the needs of new population areas and of ever more advanced buildings has meant that the State has steadily become the major partner. The partnership is known technically as the 'dual system'.

Secondary education: more for the talented

'Secondary' education, as prescribed by the Act of 1902, was not for all, nor did it mean what it means to-day. All children were entitled to 'elementary' education, whether they received it in the council schools, the voluntary schools, or independent schools for which the State had no responsibility. With some minor exceptions, it was compulsory from the age of five to fourteen. The new 'secondary' schools provided, from the age of eleven to sixteen or eighteen, more advanced studies of an academic and intellectually exacting type; at first their curriculum was largely modelled on that of the older endowed grammar schools and it offered virtually the only road, except for the children of wealthy families, to the universities. Admission to these schools was for the able children only and was by competitive examination at the age of eleven. Opportunities increased as more and more of these schools were built, but the pace of advance varied considerably between areas. The point has already been made that education is a locally based service, and the decisions about the degree of local need for secondary education and how and when to build schools to meet it was for the local education authority. Since around one-third of the education budget had to be raised through the rates (in local taxation), debate raged fiercely on local councils about what was needed and what the local ratepayers—the ordinary house-holders—could afford. Educational opportunity above the minima which legislation had prescribed came to depend on two factors: the degree of concern of local politicians and civic leaders for educational advance, and the actual material prosperity, and therefore its ability to pay, of an area.

The new secondary schools nevertheless proved themselves so forcefully that further advance became inevitable. By the 1920s, through this route, working class children were distinguishing themselves and entering universities and other forms of higher education in large numbers, and it was plain that further untapped potential must exist in those children who did not enjoy such opportunities. A committee set up by the central Board of Education under the chairmanship of a remarkably far-sighted observer, Sir Henry Hadow, reported in 1926 on primary education and in 1930 on secondary education. The first report gave considered support to trends to broaden and liberalise the elementary school curriculum. The second concerned itself with widening the opportunities for all pupils, not just the academically able, in their post-primary years of schooling. It recognised that there were practical, aesthetic and inventive talents as well as academic ones, and recommended that education should no longer take place from the age of five to fourteen in the same elementary school, but that there should be a break at eleven, at which age children who did not enter the secondary schools would transfer from a 'primary' (five to eleven) to a 'senior' (eleven to fourteen) school. This would allow buildings to be better designed and equipped for the learning characteristics of the ages in question, and in the senior schools would allow a measure of more advanced specialised teaching to take place. The Government accepted the recommendations, though the economic depression of the 1930s meant that little money for new building or equipment was available and the pace of reorganisation was uneven and generally slow. The war imposed further delay, and it was not until the 1960s that re-organisation with the break at 11 was complete.

The Post-war Period

The nation, and Parliament not least, emerged from the Second World War determined on social reform in the direction of more equal opportunity. The Education Act of 1944, passed while the war was still in progress, not only recalled and developed the aims of the Hadow Committee but activated the process of achievement. The change of school at the age of eleven was no mere pious vision but was embodied in the legislation. Children were to be educated in primary schools up to that age and then all were to transfer to secondary education. This implied a complete change in the meaning of the word *secondary*.

It now referred no longer to curriculum or to methods of teaching, but simply to age. The Act required that all pupils should be educated in accordance with their 'age, aptitude and ability'; and this clearly meant new secondary schools with new courses of practical, technical, aesthetic, physical and social content in addition to the academic 'secondary' curriculum of the past. And the Government was not prepared to wait indefinitely. The local education authorities were each required to submit for approval detailed development plans for their area with target dates. From these submissions the Ministry of Education (as it was now named) itself authorised the annual building programmes, adjudicating between the needs of areas which were in hot competition for the scarce resources of the post-war years.

In the midst of this scarcity of material resources the Minister of Education of the day, Miss Ellen Wilkinson, decided to implement in 1947 another provision of the Act, that of raising the minimum school-leaving age from fourteen to fifteen years. This decision was much attacked at the time and it did cause great difficulties of overcrowding, understaffing and—among some of the intended beneficiaries—rebellious discontent at being deprived for a year of an anticipated pay packet. In retrospect, it was almost certainly right. It stimulated feverish activity on the part of over-stretched authorities and teachers, and gave a momentum to educational change without which some of the intentions of the 1944 Act would probably still be unrealised. It was a further twenty-five years before the final stage, that of raising the minimum leaving age to sixteen years, was accomplished.

The nature of human society is such that the rainbow's end is never reached. Even while the completion of re-organisation into primary and secondary sectors was being quietly celebrated, some educationists were challenging eleven as the best transfer age—and the words *middle school* were forming on some lips. What brought this about?

CHAPTER 2

The Middle School Idea: how it arose

The foregoing sketch shows that until relatively recently the middle school was not even an idea. The Hadow Committee had recommended change of school for all at the age of eleven; the 1944 Act gave this statutory force by requiring local education authorities to arrange that children should be transferred from primary to secondary school between the ages of 10 years 6 months and 12 years. So long as this prevailed, there was little encouragement for anyone to plan alternative structures. It is true that in the small and self-contained sector of independent schools, transfer from preparatory to public school normally took place at the age of thirteen, and the usual preparatory school course ran from eight to thirteen; but the circumstances of the State and the independent school sectors were very different, and there was unfortunately too little contact between them for experiences to be effectively exchanged.

The Case for transfer at eleven

What made the Hadow Committee and the framers of the 1944 Act so sure that eleven was the right age to change school? The conclusion was not lightly reached. The Hadow members studied carefully the generally accepted experience of the day on child development and the learning processes; they listened to serving teachers and to educational thinkers; and they concluded that eleven was an age at which most children had completed the early stages of learning, had mastered the basic skills, and were ready for wider experience. They concluded also that socially and emotionally eleven year old children were ready to face change. Finally, they saw the compelling argument that, with the school leaving age set at fourteen, any later transfer age would reduce the senior school course to less than three years, and for some pupils (depending on their date of birth) to as little as four or five terms; professional opinion was united that this was too short a time to plan and implement effective senior courses. Even with the lengthening of school life by a year in prospect, the designers of the 1944 Act, led by the responsible Minister himself, R. A. (later Lord) Butler, agreed that a three year secondary course was the minimum desirable and that indeed four years would be preferable; a later transfer age than eleven would have put the hoped-for gains at risk.

Doubts about transfer at eleven

What then brought about the middle school idea? As usual, its growth was gradual, and there is no point at which we can say: this is where it began. But its beginnings certainly arose from a combination of the observations of perceptive primary school teachers and of child psychologists and paediatricians. Members of both groups, from their different standpoints, came to realise that children were nothing like as uniform in their rates of development and maturation—intellectual, social or emotional—as had been supposed; and it appeared to some that many children around the age of eleven were in fact in the grip of adolescent strains which made the age a bad one at which to impose the further strain of a change of school. This was a different picture from Hadow's; but it may be that both were right. It is commonly accepted that the onset of adolescence has come at an increasingly younger age during the past fifty years; and society itself since the war has become less stable and more disturbed in ways which react upon family life and therefore upon the experiences undergone by children. The children of to-day are not those of Sir Henry Hadow's day, and what was the wisest counsel then may not be so now. At any rate, in the 1950s the feeling grew that the issue was by no means as clear-cut as had been supposed.

The next stage was the thorough evaluation carried out by the Central Advisory Council of Education under the chairmanship of Lady Plowden. More popularly referred to as the Plowden Committee, this body was set up in 1963 by the then Minister of Education to enquire into, and to make recommendations concerning, all aspects of primary education; its report, published in 1967 under the title *Children and their Primary Schools*, advocated the reorganisation of primary education into two stages, consisting of *first schools* with an age range from four to eight and *middle schools* with an age range from eight to twelve. The educational and developmental arguments are carefully set out in the report and to very many teachers in the primary field have carried conviction.

Political considerations

In more placid times it might have been expected that the well researched recommendations of the Plowden Committee would have been left for a year or more for public and professional debate, after which the Government would have decided whether to adopt them for national implementation. Events in the secondary field had however dictated otherwise even before the report was published. When the 1944 Education Act laid down the principle of secondary education for all, it did not prescribe in what types of school the local education authorities were to meet this obligation. A handful of authorities decided even then to do so in comprehensive schools, that is, schools to which all children from the locality may proceed irrespective of ability, and in which therefore a sufficient variety of courses to give equal opportunity to all would be provided. Chief among these were Inner London (at that time the now superseded London County Council), Bristol and Coventry; and they recognised that, even with an immediate start on the planning, to build a sufficient number of large and appropriately equipped schools would absorb the likely financial resources of the next twenty years. Most authorities however acted on the generally accepted belief that it was better to provide for different levels of ability in different schools; alongside their already existing academic secondary schools, now re-named *grammar* schools, they set out to develop more practically oriented schools known as *secondary modern* schools. Here and there a few *secondary technical* schools were also set up, for bright pupils believed to have technical, rather than academic, aptitudes; in the outcome it proved impossible to separate aptitudes so precisely. Though many of the secondary modern schools had to be housed, for a while at least, in the often inadequate premises of former Hadow-type senior schools or even of unreorganised former elementary schools, nevertheless during the twenty years after the war many very fine, spacious, well equipped new schools were built, so that the aim of equality of opportunity for all pupils gradually assumed practical shape.

Despite fine performance by many of the new schools, keen controversy grew around what came to be known as the *bipartite* system. Having different types of secondary school necessarily involved selection processes at the age of eleven. In many areas the well established grammar schools had, naturally enough, greater prestige than the secondary modern schools and many anxious parents put great pressure on their children to pass into them. Similarly, some primary schools, anxious to do their best for their pupils, gave them concentrated preparation for selection tests at the expense of curricular studies proper. Finally, many children who did not qualify for the grammar schools felt an acute sense of shame.

It became obvious to many teachers, especially in the primary schools, that eleven was a very arbitrary age at which to select; they saw their pupils develop at very different rates, and some only just beginning to show their true potential at the crucial age of selection. In many circles the whole principle of selection came under challenge, and the *eleven-plus*, as the examinations were commonly known, acquired an unenviable reputation as a cause of pressure on children and of distortion of the curriculum. Moreover, on social as well as academic grounds many observers became worried about the wisdom of separating children at all during their formative teen-age years; such a practice, it was argued, was likely to perpetuate social divisions and foster class strife. Others opposed these arguments, holding especially that the able pupils, on whom the country's future depended, would be dangerously retarded in an all-abilities school. There was not, and is not to-day, an agreed public—or professional—view; but in the 1950s the Labour Party, in its quest of equality of educational opportunity for all, adopted the abolition of secondary selection as part of its political programme. When the party achieved electoral victory in 1964 and formed a government, it hastened to put this into effect.

Secondary reorganisation

The method chosen was to issue a Department of Education and Science Circular to local education authorities inviting them to submit proposals for the reorganisation, on comprehensive lines, of their secondary education. A Circular does not have statutory force but it is customary for the education service to comply with it. In this case the Department had a powerful supporting instrument in the shape of its control over the major school building programmes. This power enabled it to give priority to proposals which would advance in an area the introduction of comprehensive schools, and to withhold approval from those which did not. And, so far as buildings were concerned, the Government faced a problem; for comprehensive schools clearly had to be large to provide a range of courses sufficient for all abilities—larger than most schools then in existence. To accommodate the whole secondary school population in new buildings of an inevitably costly nature would have taken, at an optimistic estimate, until the turn of the century. Additions to existing buildings, adaptations, amalgamations and changes of use had clearly to be employed too. Acknowledging this, the DES Circular, No. 10/65 (as well known to educationists as the year 1066 to historians) offered no fewer than six acceptable ways in which authorities might re-structure their systems so as to eliminate selection.

One of these ways was to adopt a three-tier system of first, middle and upper schools in place of the familiar two-tier primary and secondary pattern. (The statutory transfer requirement was quietly forgotten; it had in fact already been modified for experimental purposes in 1964.) Its advantages were first that upper schools with a 13 to 18 age range were smaller and less costly than 11 to 18 schools, and second that existing secondary schools which were too small for use as comprehensive upper schools could be converted to middle school use. The way was thus suddenly clear for the introduction of middle schools; but not on a national scale. Five other methods of eliminating selection were also available to authorities, and the Plowden Committee's recommendation of a nation-wide structure of 8 to 12 middle schools had thereby been effectively over-ridden even before its publication eighteen months later in 1967.

Some authorities would adopt middle schools for reasons which seemed to them convincing; but many more would adhere to the age of eleven as their main transfer age. The outcome is that a patchwork of different structures is covering the country serving local needs at the expense of a co-ordinated national system. Whether this will be beneficial or not only time will tell; many parents whose work or circumstances force them to move house frequently have severe doubts. But meanwhile, the middle school is a new and deeply interesting form within the patchwork, and is worthy of close study.

To their credit, most authorities have consulted teachers and parents, in varying degrees of detail, before finally adopting a scheme—some right at the start, others only when the preparation of plans was fairly far advanced. Some parents have certainly felt that they were informed too late, or in too general a way, properly to express their anxieties; and the questions heading Chapter 1 are examples of genuine anxieties. The final decision to adopt a plan is democratically made by the local education committee and the full elected Council to which it reports; the detailed work and advice on the basis of which the decision is made is undertaken by the professional staff of the authority's education department, usually in consultation with their teachers. Many officers and elected councillors alike have been assiduous in attending parents' or public meetings to explain and be questioned about the aims and details of their scheme, and this has often given confidence to parents and sometimes led to modifications. This is not only wise but fair; if parents are to be expected to support a change which keenly affects the education of their own children, they must understand what is happening and the reasons for it. The middle school is, after all, unfamiliar ground for parents in this country, and where parental discontent with middle schools is simmering it is usually because some of the prerequisites to their introduction are missing or incomplete—additional building, staff trained in working with the new age range, proper arrangements for specially gifted children, and so on. One trend likely to emerge strengthened by the introduction of middle schools is growing parental insistence on being taken more fully into the confidence of schools, receiving more information from them and having more of a voice in choices which directly affect their children.

CHAPTER 3

Origins and practical effects

'They must upward still and onward
Who would keep abreast of truth.'
(James Russell Lowell)

'There are as yet only a handful of maintained middle schools and all are in their infancy'. These words appeared as recently as 1970 in the DES Education Pamphlet *Towards the Middle School*. The group of HM Inspectors who wrote the pamphlet nevertheless forecast that during the next decade many LEAs would adopt them; but even they must be surprised at the speed with which the handful has become a host. In January 1976, according to the most recent figures available at the time of writing, there were 1154 middle schools in England, 442,975 pupils on roll and 19,479 full-time teachers working in them, with part-timers adding the full-time equivalent of another 945. And the movement has by no means come to a halt; these numbers will continue to grow, unless the economic situation enforces a complete standstill, at least until 1980.

Definition

What exactly is a *middle school*? At first sight the term, if unimaginative, seems plain enough; it must surely identify the second of three schools through which a child will pass during the eleven or more years of his school life. The two other layers of the sandwich, usually known as *tiers*, are the *first school*, which takes pupils from the ages of 4 or 5 to 8 or 9 years, and the *upper or high schools* (other names may also be found), which take them on from the age of 12 or 13 to 18. But there are exceptions even to this simple classification. A few authorities have introduced a further break at the age of 16, giving four tiers of schooling (5 to 8, 8 to 12, 12 to 16, and 16 to 18); the purist might question whether there can be a *middle school* in a series of four, but the name seems to be accepted. Normally, the middle school is a self-contained school providing a four year course for either 8 to 12 or 9 to 13; but there are two departures from this.

Combined Schools

The first, and the more important, is the so-called *combined school*. This is a combined first and middle school, accommodating children from the age of 5 to 12 or 13—usually 12. It is almost always a former 5 to 11 primary school which now keeps its pupils a year longer, and is found either in rural areas where the number of children is not sufficient to justify separate first and middle schools, or in towns where small local primary schools had been the norm and are unlikely to be replaced for a long time yet. Many of them are voluntary, usually church, schools which were founded before the days of state participation in their areas, and which today would be unable to shoulder the cost of separate new first and middle schools—even though the DES is empowered to pay 85% of the cost of new capital building which it and the LEA approve. The combined school will therefore be with us for a long while yet, and its ultimate fate is not yet predictable. In January 1976 there were 348 of them, with somewhere between 50,000 and 60,000 pupils of middle school age and some 2,000 teachers. We shall consider later how far they can match the opportunities afforded by the larger, self-contained middle school.

Three-year schools

The second is a small group of middle schools in some north-

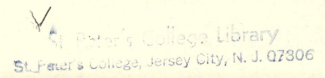

western boroughs which offer only a three-year course, from 10 to 13. There are only 35 of them, and their adoption was prompted by local factors not likely to be repeated elsewhere. Their curriculum and organisation, not surprisingly, are secondary oriented; but they will be omitted from this study when we come to consider the character and attainment of middle schools generally.

We shall of course look closely at the differences between the two main types of middle school, those from 8 to 12 and from 9 to 13, and shall try to determine whether either is to be preferred to the other. We have seen that the Plowden Committee favoured the 8 to 12 age range; but they were in fact not unsympathetic to the idea of 9 to 13, even though its upper age range lay, strictly speaking, outside their remit. Our next task is however to turn to the origins of the middle school—educational, administrative, and political.

1. EDUCATIONAL ORIGINS

We have seen how transfer at 11 came to dominate the educational scene and how, as long as it did, the middle school could not exist. We saw how to the Hadow Committee this dominant rôle was founded on more than practical expediency; it appeared justified also by the experience of educationists, especially teachers in the first generation of senior schools in reorganised areas. Not until well after 1944 was this belief questioned; and there could have been no move towards middle schools but for the widening challenge of the 1950s to both currently held views on child development and to long established teaching practices.

Internal Organisation—questions of grouping

The first practice to be questioned was really one of internal school organisation, but it reflected a rigid, even pessimistic, view of the potential of individual children. Children of primary age were educated either in all-through *primary schools* taking the full age range from 5 to 11, or in *infant schools* from 5 to 7 followed by *junior schools* from 7 to 11; these are indeed the arrangements still in use in non-middle school areas. Wherever the number of pupils permitted it, the almost invariable practice was to group children by age, with all the children of a year group in the same class. (After all, did not the 1944 Act require that children be educated by age as well as by aptitude and ability?) The size of the school did of course produce some variation, and it was not always as neat as this. In rural schools especially there might be so few children that each class would enforcedly contain children from two, three or more age groups; one class for infants and one for juniors was common, and there were even some schools in which all the children from 5 to 11 made up only a single class. In these schools teachers had clearly to prepare a variety of programmes for small groups or for single children; few lessons could be taught to the whole class, as was the standard practice in other schools. At the other end of the scale, some town schools were large enough to have two, three or even four classes for each year-group, and the common practice then was to grade the children in classes according to their ability, real or supposed. This practice was known as *streaming*, and was held to offer to both bright and slow children the best opportunity of progress. For a long while it was not regarded as disquieting that, once assigned to an A, B or C class at as early an age as seven, children rarely changed streams. This meant that a decision at the age of 7 could, at its worst, effectively deny the opportunity of passing into grammar school at 11 and on to university at 18. The claim implicit in this practice was that it was possible to make predictions about children at the age of seven which to-day most teachers would hesitate to make even much later—believing now that performance does not tell all and that potential still waits to be liberated.

In the 1950s the climate in primary schools became more shrewdly questioning for two main reasons. One was that, rather to the surprise of educationists, education itself became a subject of major and continuing public interest. The public had its own questions—not only about selection and streaming—and wanted honest and intelligible answers, not soothing syrup. The other was the post-war entry to the teaching profession of men and women older than the average training college student and with enlivening wartime experiences. Many knew from personal experience that wartime opportunities had brought out talents which their schools had never suspected. They were consequently not acquiescent lecture fodder ready to swallow easily what their trainers, head teachers and colleagues told them; they wished to experiment for themselves in teaching methods, materials and organisation. More than 40,000 of these new teachers were injected into the system through the Emergency Training Scheme (which itself mainly attracted as college tutors enterprising teachers from the schools and not from academic institutions) and they were certainly a strong factor. Along with questioning head teachers, observant inspectors and open-minded advisers, they often found in primary schools during the 1950s that the use of practical approaches, individual assignments, and discovery methods produced surprising results in the shape both of a livelier curriculum and of children more interested and better in achievement. To these teachers, and many others who sensed the trend, the assumptions on which the practices of streaming and early selection were based came increasingly under question.

Evidence from child psychologists

Support was also coming from another area. Many psychologists were becoming dubious about the view, strongly held in the 1940s and associated especially with the research and conclusions of Sir Cyril Burt, that intelligence was a general attribute transferable from one skill or attainment to another, and that in the individual it was a faculty fixed at birth and measurable. On this basis, it had been considered both practicable and fair to devise tests to measure intelligence and to grade children for educational purposes. But increasingly new evidence cast doubt upon this, while evidence from sociological and child

Just another school? In this case, a former secondary school building.

Just another school? In this case, a former junior school building.

health studies indicated that children's performance was substantially affected by such outside factors as bad home conditions or good teaching. Concern grew about the effect of environmental and social disadvantage on the educational attainments of children, and studies like those of J. W. B. Douglas demonstrated that family support and influences were of enormous importance for a child's attitudes and achievements in school.

A parallel line of enquiry, developed in particular by Douglas Pidgeon, showed that children tended to fulfil the expectations held of them, whether by family, teachers, or themselves. The expectations and attitudes of school staffs and of individual teachers appeared to him as a crucial factor—and so was school organisation. Streaming, however beneficial to the able in giving them high expectations of themselves, was virtually certain to depress the performance of the other children. Many teachers who believed this went on to demonstrate that it was possible to organise classes so that several different kinds and grades of work could go on side by side in the same room; this demolished the major argument in favour of streaming. So strongly and completely did the convictions of practising teachers change that, in a few short years in the 1960s, streaming virtually disappeared from one area after another. If to-day it survives at all, it can only be in a few backwaters out of touch with the main stream of educational thought.

In this new climate it was inevitable also that some would question whether the age of 11 really was a natural and beneficial one at which to transfer children from one school to another, or whether this belief was after all a rationalisation of historical accident and administrative convenience. The next step was to consider alternatives; the pros and cons of middle schools were therefore soon under active discussion, to such effect that by the early 1960s it was not merely the idea that was being examined, but actual plans which were being formulated. By 1963 a number of forward-looking LEAs were doing this—the West Riding of Yorkshire, Hull, Bradford and Wallasey in particular.

Changes in the approach to teaching

The second practice (or perhaps group of practices) to undergo both challenge and change was the whole amalgam of teaching methods, techniques, and classroom organisation which in the primary schools set the scene for children learning. A gradual revolution was taking place, founded upon the same kind of close observation and study of how children naturally learned and matured which was leading to the organisational changes within schools just outlined. There was no closely organised movement, with leaders and slogans; rather, in different parts of the country head teachers, training college tutors, inspectors and advisers came to believe and to say the same things, to put them into practice locally and to pool their knowledge as opportunity arose. One such network arose quite spontaneously from the series of short courses for infant heads and others run over many years by a redoubtable member of H.M. Inspectorate, Miss Jennie Mack; the enthusiasm generated on these courses was such that some follow-up groups formed by members at the time were still in existence twenty years later. Though follow-up was less marked, similar courses directed by her colleague in the junior field, Christian Schiller, had the same spearhead quality.

The move to relate teaching methods and programmes to children's actual learning processes, rather than to a sequential arrangement of knowledge in neatly divided theoretical subjects, began in a handful of infant schools in the 1940s; in differing degrees, the child-based patterns and practices to which it led are now near universal in infant and first schools. During the 1950s they spread upwards into the junior schools or years, so successfully that by the middle 1960s the Plowden Committee estimated that throughout the country one-third of all primary schools were completely committed to child-centred approaches and a further one-third were affected in some degree. Infant teachers especially were instrumental in this, spending much of their time watching what children actually did when offered particular resources (sand, water, climbing

frames, counting apparatus, simple musical instruments, con-
structional toys, games, books) and on the basis of what they
saw leading them to new learning experiences for which they
appeared to be ripe. This approach did not usually displace
direct teaching, but linked it with what was immediate and
interesting in the child's own experience. The child who liked
talking found his desire encouraged and the vocabulary he used
systematically enlarged; the one who was attracted to books
was taught to read and led to yet more books; the one who
wished to listen to stories, act them, write, sing or paint about
them, found the opportunity given, with encouragement from
the teacher to do it a little better than the day or the week
before and from time to time to do it with other children instead
of alone.

This account simplifies what is a complex process, for no
child progresses day by day at an exactly uniform rate, and child
interests, especially in the junior years, may rise and fade at a
speed which needs some tempering from the teacher. Teaching
of this kind calls for great skill, especially when the responsibility of the teacher is for 35 children or more, and not just for
a single child. But the movement went steadily forward and in
due time received the accolade of convinced approval from the
Plowden Committee. Though it still arouses some controversy
in educational circles, one of the most significant signs to the
professional observer is that few teachers who have tried these
approaches ever seem to go back to the more formal teaching of
earlier years, and those who do are the least resourceful.

This change of mood, following the challenges to previously
established beliefs and practices, came at the right time to
influence the middle school. The educational leaders who
actually set up the earliest middle schools did so with the deliberate aim of prolonging the new child-centred approaches to
teaching and learning beyond the age of eleven, being convinced that most children would benefit from a later introduction to the more systematically structured secondary
approaches. Prominent among these leaders was Sir Alec Clegg,
the humane and imaginative Chief Education Officer of the

West Riding, and it is significant that he was in constant educational dialogue with his teachers.

Even before this, many infant teachers were advocating delaying the transfer of pupils from their schools to the juniors until the age of eight, mainly to permit the slower or backward children to master skills, their grasp of which, at the age of seven, was uncertain and easily set back. The adoption of a first and middle school structure translated both these aspirations into reality; and what it meant was that, as seen in areas like the West Riding, the middle school would continue the primary mode of teaching and learning. In the areas which prepared for their middle schools in this way, it is no surprise to find that many of the chosen head teachers were men and women who were themselves committed to these same approaches and who welcomed the opportunity to prolong the practice of them.

2. ADMINISTRATIVE ORIGINS

The principal administrative advantage of the middle school, ironically, was the saving in size which it made possible in comprehensive secondary schools. It has already been stated that, in the wake of the 1944 Education Act, a mere handful of authorities decided to build comprehensive schools; most remained committed to the bi-partite system of grammar and secondary modern schools. But in the 1950s and early 1960s the tide of opinion moved steadily, if slowly, in favour of comprehensives. The chief worry of many teachers and authorities was their size, for it was then considered that, in order to support in their sixth forms (from 16 to 18) the range of advanced work which the grammar schools had offered, a school of 1500 to 2000 pupils would be necessary; anything smaller would produce advanced courses of only two and three pupils each. But the problems caused by sheer size soon became apparent; many pupils felt that the schools were vast and impersonal, and it was very difficult for the staff to maintain good pastoral care and personal contact, especially with the less confident or more rebellious pupils. But, if the 11 and 12 year olds could remain in middle schools, the size of an otherwise 2000 strong comprehensive was reduced by 600 or so pupils at a stroke—a substantial reason for supporting a three-tier system with middle schools.

The way had been pointed, years before the first middle school, by the Leicestershire education authority, and its motive was similar. The aim of the Leicestershire plan, formulated by its Director of Education, Stewart Mason, and introduced in stages from 1957 onwards, was to re-organise the county's secondary education on comprehensive lines without either contravening the statutory requirement to transfer pupils at 11 or embarking on huge programmes of new building. This was accomplished by splitting secondary education into two tiers at the age of 14 and by adapting all existing secondary schools, grammar and modern, in a locality for use in either the lower or upper tier. At the age of 11, therefore, pupils moved from their primary into junior high schools. After three years in them, all those who intended to stay at school until at least 16 moved again to the senior high schools which had an age range from 14 to 18 years; the remainder, a minority, stayed on in the junior high schools for their final year. Comprehensive education was thus provided within roughly the existing stock of buildings.

This Leicestershire plan did not involve true middle schools, which were not possible within the statutory framework of the time; the schools were secondary in staffing, organisation and outlook. Nor did it become a widely copied precedent, though it did later rank as one of the six acceptable choices offered to authorities in the DES Circular 10/65. But it did demonstrate that a three-tier organisation was both possible and workable, and, in addition to attracting a lot of attention overseas as well as at home, it helped to pave the way administratively for the middle school.

It no doubt also helped to encourage other LEAs to prepare schemes of reorganisation. The West Riding did this as early as 1963 for one of its Divisional Executives (the area south-east of

Wakefield), adopting a three-tier system of 5 to 9 first schools, 9 to 13 middle schools, and 13 to 18 upper schools. Similar studies were taking place in Hull, Bradford (where building difficulties were intense), Wallasey (where the best use of available buildings was the starting point) and more tentatively in some other areas. Approaches were made to the Minister of Education, Sir Edward Boyle, for relaxation of the statutory transfer requirement. The outcome was the Education Act of 1964, a modest measure which authorised for experimental purposes the establishment of a small unspecified number of schools straddling the junior and secondary age ranges. This was a cautious measure, and one which opened no flood-gates; but it showed that the government of the day was not opposed to experiment where a substantial body of educational opinion and experience supported it. Administrative action in favour of middle schools had received an amber, if not yet a green, light.

3. POLITICAL ORIGINS

Two years later, following the change of government in 1964, came the full green light already touched on in the previous chapter. The new Labour government lost no time in announcing its intention to eliminate selection and to introduce comprehensive secondary schools nation-wide. Almost overnight the middle school became a valuable agent, in certain circumstances, of advancing the process of 'going comprehensive'. DES Circular 10/65 put the matter beyond doubt in ending the relevant paragraph with the words:

> *The establishment of middle schools with age ranges of 8 to 12 or 9 to 13 has an immediate attraction in the context of secondary reorganisation on comprehensive lines.*

It was certainly political motives which gave this impetus to the spread of middle schools; but we have examined their strong educational justification, and there is surely no discredit in adopting an educationally sound programme because it happens also to suit a political one. In fact, both the choice of the six acceptable methods on which authorities might base their plans, and the approval of LEAs' individual plans, were made by the Secretary of State, Antony Crosland, with the most careful regard to educational consequences. Dispassionate observation of the actual achievement of the schools approved in the early days certainly shows few disasters among the middle schools, whatever view may be taken of the comprehensive schools which they feed.

Supporters of the middle school movement may well be grateful for the political impetus, for without it progress would have been slow indeed. The educational rationale, and the professional experience of leaders like Sir Alec Clegg, were known to ministers, and there is no reason to regret that it was a politically motivated decision which actually opened the way to middle school expansion. The motives in question in no way conflict with the educational aims of the enlightened middle school.

What then is the middle school?

So what is the middle school? Factually, it is a school with a four year age range bridging the gap between primary and secondary ages and—more important—their approaches to learning. Put thus baldly, it may not sound a very startling development and might be dismissed as a mere piece of organis-ational tinkering. But we have seen that the causes of its introduction lie deep. It is, educationally speaking, a vehicle for using to the best advantage our much increased knowledge of how children develop, learn and mature in these formative years; for taking fresh looks at the nature of human knowledge and the ways in which it can most profitably be moulded into the curriculum; for eliminating the setbacks which many children suffered from transfer at ages when they were not ready for it; and for bringing primary and secondary teachers to appreciate each the outlook of the other, and to see the educational process as a whole. If it really achieves these objectives, we should be grateful indeed.

CHAPTER 4

A distinctive framework

Though Shakespeare ask us: What's in a name?
As if cognomens were much the same,
There's really a very great scope in it . . .
(Tom Hood)

Are there distinctive characteristics about the new middle schools
– or are they, as so many people felt after the last war about the
first secondary modern schools, merely a new title disguising
what was there before? The answer is a firm: yes, there are
distinctive characteristics, and no, it is not the previous school
renamed in order to fool a trusting public; not, at any rate,
where the transformation has been carefully prepared and
smoothly executed. Complete uniformity would be foreign to
the English temperament and will not be found; nor will a
fixed and final identity, for these are early years, and the schools
are still testing the ground. But a distinctive framework may
certainly be discerned as one looks at middle schools as a whole.

(1) Variety: the local flavour

Rather more than in the primary and secondary schools of
the country, middle schools seem to reflect local and perhaps
regional attitudes. The middle schools in Bradford or Wakefield
have a flavour and a personality quite different from those in
Suffolk or Somerset. It is partly that the outlook of the region
has stamped itself upon the new institution, perhaps even more
that preparation has been a genuinely local affair and that far

more teachers and other practising professionals have had a voice in the undertaking than in any previous reorganisation. Those who believe that regional characteristics and life styles are good and should be preserved will welcome this. Individual schools of course vary, as they always will; but there can be a closer kinship with the school in the same authority twenty miles away than with one down the road which is across an authority boundary, and which is the product of a different preparatory experience.

(2) *Local decision and the rôle of the DES*

We have already seen that the decision to set up middle schools is essentially a local one, even though government action was necessary to make it possible. The same is true of what the local middle schools are to become. The DES lays down no obligatory guidelines. Its three relevant publications (apart from the administrative Circulars such as No. 10/65) are written by professional educationists and design teams; they embody much useful thought and experience but there is no obligation on authorities or teachers to follow it or even to read it.

Two of them were written by specialist members of HM Inspectorate and are the fruit of partnership between themselves, LEA officers, and teachers. *Towards the Middle School* (1970) assessed possible organisational developments inside the schools, discussed approaches in the field of curriculum and method, and identified requirements of accommodation, staffing, training and management. (Already it is clear that the rather cautious requirements adumbrated, especially as regards staffing, were too low, and many authorities have in practice been more generous.) This pamphlet was, so to speak, a textbook of theory and philosophy for the middle school.

Launching Middle Schools, published at the same time, was a complementary operational case study of the introduction of middle schools in one area of the old West Riding. Based on Inspectorate surveys carried out with the full co-operation of the Chief Education Officer and the schools, it described the hard experience of planning, designing, equipping, training and finally opening and running the middle schools. It identified the many problems in such an operation and hinted at the enormous amount of detail inseparable from change on this scale; it ended with an encouraging assessment of the benefits already conferred upon the pupils in the first year of working.

The third publication was actually a forerunner, for it appeared in 1966 before any middle schools were actually built. Under the title *Middle Schools* (sub-titled *New Problems in School Design: Implications of transfer at 12 or 13 years*) it boldly tackled the question of the types of design of school buildings which would give most scope and flexibility to the middle schools which it was then certain would come. It was prepared by a design team in the DES Architects' and Buildings' Branch of which two experienced HMIs were members. Its starting point therefore was the kind of educational approaches likely to be appropriate to middle schools, and its keynote was flexibility. After this brief introduction it set out a number of possible designs for new purpose-built middle schools, for extensions to existing primary schools to equip them for their new rôle, and in an appendix outlined a plan for an actual school (Delf Hill, Bradford) which was shortly afterwards built by the LEA for experimental purposes. This Building Bulletin (No. 35) came at a crucial moment for many authorities and was widely studied, though unhappily it assumed more generous cost limits than have since prevailed.

Some authorities, like the two mentioned above, consulted widely with the professional wings of the DES, with curriculum development agencies (though these were nothing like as familiar a part of the educational scene as they are now), and with university departments of education and teacher training colleges. Others lacked the time, and sometimes the desire, to do this. Either way the ultimate decisions were taken locally. In some areas teachers complained bitterly of lack of consultation at what, in their eyes, was in the last resort a professional matter, since it was they who had to do the teaching and who had no heart for it in the absence of adequate resources or of proper

time to prepare themselves for new teaching rôles. It is significant that most of the authorities who introduced middle schools
early had spent years preparing—eight or nine years, for
example, in both Hull and the West Riding. The stages of
preparation typically ran something like this:

   (i) determining the overall provision for the area
  (ii) determining the future rôle of individual schools
 (iii) determining the necessary construction programmes,
      both of new schools and extensions
 (iv) planning the parallel provision of furnishings and
      equipment
  (v) setting up working parties on curricular and organis-
      ational matters, together with preliminary in-service
      training programmes for teachers
 (vi) calculating staffing establishments and arranging for the
      re-deployment of teachers, so far as possible honouring
      individual preferences
(vii) informing parents and the public of the aims and
      progress of the plans and promoting dialogue with them.

These stages naturally overlapped, and the amount of work
involved was prodigious. These tasks, however much consultation might be available from other quarters, were wholly
local; and it is therefore easily understandable that, in the areas
where they really flourish, middle schools are a truly local
creation and do reflect the characteristics and flavour of the
locality.

(3) *Grouping of Schools*

Primary and secondary teachers were brought together, often
for the first time and certainly in ways previously unknown,
when they tackled the implications for their own work of the
intended middle schools in the working parties referred to in (v)
above. Where this consultation was satisfying and effective
there was strong impetus to continue it even after the middle
schools opened; after all, they shared many of the same problems. A natural grouping which arose in some places (and could

in almost all) was that of the upper school and those middle schools which contributed pupils to it. A community of interest can then be fostered, and a measure of agreement possibly reached by all the schools within the group on such matters as record-keeping, aspects of school routine, conventions over the marking of written work, and liaison with parents. Even if they agree to differ, there is still value in each knowing what the differences are. In some areas joint occasions take place, such as plays and concerts in which staff and pupils from both upper and middle schools join.

(4) *The Size of Schools: some critical factors*

It is curious that, although controversy has raged over the size of secondary schools, middle schools have aroused far less debate. Possibly this is because people have not felt outraged by the proposals which authorities have put forward for approval by the DES in the same way that many were by the proposals for mammoth secondary schools. If this is so, it must be that an instinct about size has kept proposals within reason, or else that the sites and buildings converted to middle school use themselves imposed a limit. Is there an optimum size? It is certainly possible to identify sizes which are too small or too large; and if there is an optimum, it lies somewhere between. In determining the size of a school, there are three general factors which should be taken into account: the response of children to size, the economic use of staff, and the effectiveness of different types of building.

(a) RESPONSE OF CHILDREN

While individual children do of course vary considerably in the size of the school they can either tolerate or enjoy, it is broadly true that the younger the child, the smaller (and so less frightening or bewildering) should be the school he is in. Much experienced opinion in the primary world has long considered a school of 300 pupils the maximum desirable, and has been uncompromisingly opposed to schools of 500 or more. This runs for schools in which the youngest children may be only 5 and the eldest 11 years of age. In middle schools, where the youngest are 8 or 9 and the eldest 12 or 13, children should be able to adapt themselves to being part of a considerably larger community; the 13 year old children in fact may positively profit by the opportunities for leadership and influence which a larger school can give them. There would seem to be no strong objection, on grounds of social atmosphere or of school organisation, to middle schools of 500 to 600. This is not to minimise the effect of the quality of the head's leadership and of the corporate personality of the staff. Ultimately it is they who create a stable atmosphere and good relationships; but the size of the school may either help or hinder.

(b) THE ECONOMIC EMPLOYMENT OF STAFF

The staff are there to teach, and curriculum and organisation are therefore of major importance. These aspects are studied later, but for the moment it can be assumed that no single teacher, however well informed, can master the knowledge needed for middle school work in every subject of the curriculum. There is also a distinct advantage in every subject having one teacher with some special knowledge of it. A glance at present-day needs in languages, mathematics, science, social studies, religious and moral education, art and various crafts, domestic subjects and physical education makes it plain that a staff of a dozen is the minimum required to meet them—and this leaves no margin (for it cannot be assumed that new or replacement appointments will always neatly bring in teachers with the exact balance of subjects required). Allowing this necessary margin for manoeuvre, and assuming a staffing ratio of around one teacher to 20 pupils, a figure of some 300 pupils is an effective minimum. This is not to say that a smaller school cannot operate, but it will probably have to offer a more restricted curriculum or to cut back on special arrangements for groups of pupils such as the backward or the very able. A school twice this size could be very fortunately placed over staffing, for it could, for instance, appoint two or three science teachers, each strong in a different branch of science, and could widen its treatment of science in consequence. There are many ways of organising staff internally which will be considered later; for the moment, we can accept that schools with rolls of between 300 and 600 pupils have the opportunity both to recruit and to use staff effectively. Smaller schools inevitably face some curricular limitation unless their staffs are expensively large.

(c) THE USE OF BUILDINGS

There is a great variety of middle school buildings, new and old, specially designed and painfully adapted, former primary and former secondary, attractive and austere.

In designing a new school, the team entrusted with the task will try to provide a building in which all reasonable needs of the curriculum in the shape of classrooms, laboratories, art and craft rooms, gymnasium, music and visual aids rooms, and so on can be met within the permitted cost. (This cost is fixed by the DES and authorities have to keep within it; its basis is in effect a given cost figure for the number and ages of pupils for whom the school is approved. It is of course adjusted from time to time, but adjustments lag behind increases in costs.) It is the practical and specialist teaching spaces such as laboratories, workshops and assembly hall which are the most costly, and a minimum of six or eight of these is desirable to cover all needs; in a small school with fewer spaces, there has to be some shared use. Skilled design teams normally succeed in providing two specialist spaces for each 100 or so pupils, and on this calculation 300 to 400 pupils allow a well equipped middle school to be provided. Above this figure, additional spaces can be designed for branches of art, and gains may still be made in catering for crafts, music practice rooms, language teaching with audio-visual courses, and so on. An 8 to 12 school needs less than a 9 to 13 in the way of costly specialist spaces; but its approved cost figure for building purposes is reduced accordingly.

Adapting or extending schools originally built for another purpose has to be more pragmatic. The design team will still try to meet the same curricular needs, but may be restricted by the nature of the already existing buildings and the money available; sound buildings cannot be dispensed with because they are not entirely in accord with current ideas. In 8 to 12 areas, the buildings to be adapted or extended are usually primary schools, often of older traditional type consisting of a hall, classrooms, maybe one or more prefabricated classrooms on or across the playground, and little else. Sometimes there is no room to enlarge the site, and in these cases considerable ingenuity is necessary to provide even some of the additional activities likely to be found in newly designed schools. Where there is room, many authorities add separate system-built rooms, often known as *conversion units*; they are usually rather larger than normal classrooms and are equipped with basic services (water, drainage and electricity) and they prove adaptable to different curricular uses such as handicraft, domestic crafts, art or science according to the current need of the school. A middle school needs more than just classroom accommodation, but clearly money spent on additions has to be justified in terms of the number of pupils. Any middle school, however small, must have one or two such additional rooms; but in practice it is rarely economic to provide a pair of these rooms for numbers much below 300—unless of course the number of classrooms is inadequate for the projected number of pupils. In a few cases the primary schools to be adapted are relatively new and built on the more open, flexible lines which have become common in the last twenty years; here the task is easier.

For the 9 to 13 age range, small secondary schools, not large enough for comprehensive upper schools, are often designated for middle school use. These of course already contain specialist rooms such as laboratory, art room, handicraft and domestic science rooms, a gymnasium or combined hall/gymnasium, and perhaps others too. Here the problem has often been to adapt the rather rigid designs of most of these schools to permit easier circulation, working in small groups, free as well as formal teaching methods, and possibly the introduction of additional subjects. The problems are interesting and many authorities' design teams have produced ingenious and effective solutions. So far as size is concerned, these former secondary schools were rarely designed for fewer than 300 to 400 pupils, and as middle schools they are not likely to house smaller rolls than this.

In terms of size, the expected difference between 8 to 12 and 9 to 13 schools emerges strongly from the DES figures for January 1976. Two-thirds of all the 8 to 12 schools have between 200 and 400 pupils, and it is a fair deduction that authorities have accepted this as their distinctive size and that variations from it are largely due to special circumstances—restricted sites, thinly populated areas, or the accommodation actually available in buildings taken over from another purpose. Only 49 of the 8 to 12 schools have fewer than 200 pupils, and only 17 have more than 600. The spread is greater with the 9 to 13 schools, where there is a remarkably even spread of schools with rolls of between 200 and 600. The actual break-down shows 80 schools with rolls between 200 and 300, 119 between 300 and 400, 107 between 400 and 500, and 82 between 500 and 600—an almost perfect distribution curve over this age spread! Only 19 are recorded with fewer than 200 pupils, but a further 76 have more than 600, of which two only exceed the 800 pupil figure (and in both of these site difficulties in a built-up area were responsible.)

In practice, therefore, planning authorities have settled less on an optimum size than on the most convenient size locally within an acceptable range; and the ranges in question do so far generally satisfy the basic needs concerned with children, staff and buildings.

The resources for learning; a library corner.

Space at a premium; but learning goes on.

CHAPTER 5

The Opportunities

Instruction which is not progressive, while it may be of some use as drill and discipline, is of little real educational value. It gives only a superficial and transitory acquirement, while at the same time it fails to interest or to stimulate the scholar.

(Prefatory Memorandum to the Regulations for Secondary Schools, Board of Education, 1904)

There is a tide in the affairs of men
Which, taken at the flood, leads on to fortune.
(William Shakespeare)

Perhaps there is a tide in the affairs of schools also, for it is men and women who make schools what they are, and children are the raw material on which they work; children growing, learning, maturing, developing their potential in measure as they are given opportunity, guidance and encouragement to do so. The middle schools have the opportunity to set up a new educational experience for these children, in which acquirements (a vanished but expressive word!) can be not just transitory and superficial, but progressive throughout a critically formative age range, one in which hitherto progress has had to surmount, if it could, the great divide of change of school at the age of 11. This new experience can do three things: bridge the gap at 11, harmonise primary and secondary modes of teaching and learning, and in so doing assert the underlying continuity of the educational process, a process which for the child ought to be unbroken.

41

Bridging the Gap: the Nature of the Task

One day in the early 1960s an experienced inspector was heard to remark that, if a visitor from Mars spent one day in a typical English primary school and the next in a typical secondary school, he would be tempted to believe that he was on two different planets. This remark, more wistful than harsh, reflected the wide differences in aims, methods, organisation and relationships as they appeared to a friendly observer familiar with both. Some of the differences are natural and right because of the different ages and degree of maturity of the pupils; others are less beneficial and are hallowed by custom rather than by reason. The brief sketch in the opening chapter showed that primary and secondary education in this country differed in their origins, their history, and their purposes; they travelled along lines which were far apart and only in recent years has real understanding between the two sectors begun to grow.

If anything, the changes which came over primary education in the post-1944 years widened the gap, at least for a while. Those primary schools which accepted the concept of child-centred learning and which helped their pupils to learn through discovery processes, active engagement, and individual assignments found that a gulf divided them from the traditional primary schools which were pursuing subject-centred learning through class teaching, and even more from the specialised teaching practices of traditional secondary schools. The new primary schools set out to help children learn in the ways which came most easily to them as individuals; to accustom them to work on their own for substantial periods of time; at the end of a task, to choose their own occupation without wasteful queueing for fresh instructions from the teacher; to co-operate with groups of their fellow-pupils for various purposes; to browse freely among the books, pictures, maps, film loops and other resources available to them; to refer for information or advice not necessarily to one teacher only but to members of a team; to form the habit of observation and enquiry, taking an interest in their environment and in the world beyond; to look critically at their own and at other pupils' work; to range widely in order to discover their own particular talents, whether of intellect, creative artistry, or physical prowess; and to learn how to learn rather than simply to master a given block of knowledge.

All this led to routines, practices and relationships very different from those in the secondary schools. Here the aims were to foster a disciplined approach to learning; the ability to follow exact instructions, to memorise and apply formulae; to present work, especially written work, according to certain conventions; to work through prescribed syllabuses and to master in sequence given blocks of knowledge, without digressing on individual lines of enquiry or attractive side issues. The requirements of the public examinations, mainly the Ordinary level syllabuses of the General Certificate of Education, exerted a strong influence on the work in many schools years before the age of 16 at which they were normally taken; sometimes the shadow fell even over the first year pupils fresh from primary school.

To a pupil, the change could be startling. Instead of the lightweight stackable furniture and the informal, easily changed groupings of the primary class, the new pupil in the secondary school found himself in formally ranged rows of desks or tables. Instead of having the freedom of his classroom, wing or even school, able for much of the day to leave his place and go off to consult books or resources elsewhere, he was expected to remain at his desk unless specific permission to move were given. Instead of being free for large blocks of time to pursue an individual assignment or to work at a group project, maybe for a whole morning or afternoon, he found the day neatly chopped up into 40 minute periods with the change-over announced by bells. Instead of being able to turn to one teacher or to members of a small team when he needed help, he might find that teacher followed teacher through a seven or eight period day but that none evinced much interest in what any of the others were doing. Relationships too were inevitably more formal, however friendly the individual teachers. The specialist teaching approach which put him in contact with several teachers in the course of a day gave little time for informal conversation; moreover, there was a recognised hierarchy of teachers and taught, orders given and obeyed. Echoing the Poet Laureate, he might have said that he was summoned by bells and dismissed by bells—though one often unwelcome acquisition at the end of day would be a ration of homework, sometimes testing new ground but often recapitulating what he had already done.

It is small wonder if the change came as a shock to some pupils and a cause of numbed bewilderment to others, especially those from small schools. Many suffered setbacks in their learning and in their social attitudes. At worst, some slow learners or pupils lacking in confidence were so affected that they never recovered but became the truants or the illiterates of later years.

The contrast has been stated in extreme, but not uncommon, terms. There were of course many secondary schools where things were done very differently, many where curriculum reform was leading to more practical and more individual work and to less rigid and less specialist organisations in the early years. The sharpness of the contrast was rarely intended, but was due far less often to prejudice than to sheer ignorance in both sectors of what really happened in the other. Lifting the veil sometimes had dramatic effects, as at a conference in a large borough in the early 1960s where some seventy teachers who had spent three days in each others' schools came together for a final day and the proceedings for some time took on the air of a confessional, as primary teachers stated their regret at not having better prepared their pupils for the transfer and (in greater numbers) secondary teachers expressed shock and remorse at the way they had underestimated their pupils' capabilities and at the drudgery they had been inflicting on many who, a few weeks earlier in their primary schools, had been producing work of a quality and diversity that they had not dreamed of.

The middle school opportunity is to ease this transition by accustoming their older children over a period to the learning practices they will meet in their next school and on which they can well embark before transfer. There are many:- to study in depth; to the making of reasoned choices in preparation for the fuller specialisation of the upper schools; to disciplined present-ation of work without abandoning their creative impulses, whether in language, the arts, music, dance or drama; to planning their own work ahead, to accepting more structured working patterns and more detailed critical appraisal. Such pro-grammes need, of course, to be matched by a willingness on the part of the upper schools to join with the middle schools in discussion of the issues involved and to prepare themselves for the kind of pupils they will eventually receive.

Primary and Secondary Approaches: can the Middle School harmonise them?

The Plowden Committee, convinced that 11 was too young an age for general transfer of pupils, considered very carefully the rival merits of 12 and 13. The Committee gave resounding approval to the new philosophy and methods which had been steadily spreading in primary schools and was anxious that these should form the basis of work in the new middle schools which it advocated. In a key paragraph (383) their report went on:

> If the middle school is to be a new and progressive force, it must develop further the curriculum, methods and attitudes which exist at present in junior schools. It must move forward into what is now regarded as secondary school work, but it must not move so far away that it loses the best of primary education as we know it now. The extended programme will require teachers with a good grasp of subject matter, but we do not want the middle school to be dominated by secondary school influences. Clearly these aims could be achieved with transfer set at either 12 or 13.

This is true; but the two types of school will not be the same. Both have in fact flourished; in January 1976 there were 631 schools with the 8 to 12 age range and 483 with 9 to 13. The 8 to 12 school is almost bound to be firmly rooted in the kind of primary practice which so commended itself to the Plowden Committee; the 9 to 13 school has the greater opportunity to introduce its pupils to the modes of work and thought just referred to.

The Approach in the 9 to 13 School

If the 9 to 13 school is to succeed in this task, it must achieve continuity. No school is likely to be a satisfactory educational institution if it contents itself with borrowing two years of its course from the primary school (however enlightened) followed by two years from the secondary school. It has been said that such a school would display about as much originality and positive initiative as a pantomime horse, in which there is little real identity of purpose between front and back legs.

The four year course must be designed as an evolving whole, in which changing modes of teaching and learning and a gradual concentration of studies in depth are matched by careful consideration of the part which each teacher can best play, of the degree of specialist teaching desired at successive year levels, and of the right priorities in the use of the accommodation and the choice of equipment. The design of the whole course needs to be understood by the whole staff, even if some of them teach only in one or two of the year groups, so that the purpose of their own contribution in the unfolding process is clear. Only with a philosophy and structure of this kind can the 9 to 13 middle school evolve its own identity and make its distinctive contribution.

Within this framework, the Plowden guidance is certainly right. The curriculum, methods and attitudes which have justified themselves in the junior schools must exercise a strong influence. But other factors must also be taken into account. Generations of pupils entering secondary schools at the age of 11 have benefited from specialist staffing and accommodation in a whole range of subjects—physical education, a foreign language, laboratory science, wood and metalwork, home economics and the domestic crafts. Very rarely could primary schools match these opportunities, and that the Plowden Committee was not against them is shown by the satisfaction with which they recorded the enlargement of the primary school curriculum in some of these directions. Most of the country's children still enter secondary schools at 11; let the middle schools by all means approach these areas of the curriculum differently, but they must not contemplate starving their pupils of opportunity which their fellows of the same age elsewhere enjoy.

A further factor they have to consider is the apprehension felt by some upper schools because they now have pupils for only three years before the usual public examinations' age instead of five. There is a case for regarding this as liberation rather than as imposing a handicap, for some nervous or unimaginative teachers in secondary schools subject their pupils to barren pre-examination drills long before they need; in contrast, the middle schools have the opportunity for two years of stimulating work beyond the age of 11 without this shadow falling across it. Nevertheless, good middle schools will wish to ease the transition at 13 by close contact with their upper schools and by agreeing on a measure of ground which it is both useful for the pupils and helpful to the upper schools to cover; there is after all no point in getting rid of the risks of transfer at 11 only to substitute a fresh hazard at 13.

There is so much that is admirable in both the primary and secondary traditions that schools which can harmonise them, drawing on the best of both and making appropriate combinations of them, can render a great service. That there are some will be seen in Chapter 6. Good schools in the 9 to 13 age range can in fact be either primary or secondary based, so long as they respect the other tradition also, and regard it as complementary to their own, drawing upon it appropriately and naturally. Here lies the greatest opportunity of the 9 to 13 middle school.

The Approach in the 8 to 12 School

If the task of the 8 to 12 middle school appears superficially easier, it has none the less pitfalls to avoid. One is that the temptation to hard-pressed authorities to give it less in the way of facilities than it needs can be considerable, and indeed some 8 to 12 schools have received very little more than they already had as 7 to 11 junior schools. This is a particular risk where the schools are small, as in some rural areas, or cannot be enlarged, as in some urban ones. The Plowden Committee had an allied anxiety, on this score, that advancing the transfer age by one year only ran the risk of not confronting teachers forcefully enough with the challenge to think afresh about their 12 year old pupils. Experience in schools which have risen to this challenge shows that pupils in this final year not only mature beyond what had been expected of them but show themselves able to take responsibility in a way which would hardly have come their way as first year pupils in a secondary school. When they are encouraged to undertake imaginative and demanding work, its quality is sometimes astonishing; and the pupils' gain in both personality and attainment is very marked. Their tastes and abilities are diverging; their preferences and persuasions are becoming more evident; their intellectual capacities sometimes positively leap ahead.

To make full use of the 8 to 12 age range means far more than thinking in terms of an extra year's programme. Work in this final year must follow logically from what has preceded it, must build on the habits of enquiry and the abilities for individual work formed in the earlier years, and must both exploit knowledge already gained and introduce new elements. For slow learners or weak pupils, the final year may indeed be valuable in consolidating what has already been done and in establishing confidence; but able pupils become bored or fretful if they lack new material, new problems and new opportunities to explore their talents of reasoning and creativity. Some of the smaller middle schools and combined schools have found this a real difficulty, especially if there are a mere handful of such pupils. The case for additional resources and for special training of some teachers is strong.

The rôle of the middle schools, if they succeed in grasping the opportunities outlined in this chapter, is that of catalyst, pioneer and trailblazer. Probably around one child in every five in the appropriate age groups is now in a middle school. The figure is far from negligible, but it is still a minority. The direction taken by the country's education system later in this century may however depend on the experience of these very middle schools now at work. Among them are innovators and experimenters, visionaries and realists. In Part 2 we take a look at a cross section of them in the attempt to form an overall view of how they are faring.

PART II

INSIDE THE SCHOOLS

CHAPTER 6

Some Typical Middle Schools

'By their fruits ye shall know them'

The great variety that exists among middle schools in size, nature, buildings, staffing, objectives and approaches has already been stressed. The purpose of this chapter is to give the reader, through half-a-dozen typical examples, a bird's eye view of the different kinds of middle school that are to be found to-day; and, if the accounts provoke searching questions, so much the better. The method chosen is a little unusual. Instead of the more familiar method of giving faithful portraits of actual schools, what is presented is six composite examples of schools of the various main types; each draws upon several broadly similar schools in order to show, in the finished composition, most if not all of the characteristics and practices widely found in schools of the particular type. All six schools portrayed are fictitious, in the strict sense of the word; but they are genuine documentary in the sense that nothing is mentioned in any account which cannot be found typically and frequently in schools of the kind described. It is hoped that this approach will give a more widely representative picture of the overall middle school situation to-day, warts and all, than would be possible otherwise, even if a little of the excitement which arises from reading solely of the work of outstanding and unusual—though not necessarily typical—schools is sacrificed in the process.

School A	*Name:*	Aurora Middle School
	Location:	London Borough of Townleigh
	Age range:	8 to 12
	Roll:	380. Now in its fourth year.

Area served

A typical London suburb, mainly working class, with the emphasis on skilled or semi-skilled labour; most mothers work full or part time. Substantial number of one-parent families. One medium-sized council housing estate and a large area of older terraced property, most of it well maintained. Approximately one-fifth of the pupils from a pleasant middle class area; many very bright. A second fifth from overseas families of many nationalities, the largest groups being Indian, and Asian from

Uganda and Kenya; some language problems in these groups but parental support good.

Premises

The school was built seven years ago as a 3 form entry (ie having three classes in each year) junior school, but re-organisation was already in prospect and it was designed with eventual middle school use in mind. The Authority had a consultative group on school design on which administrators, architects and teachers worked together; the present head was a member and his ideas were influential on the design. It is therefore in effect a purpose built middle school based on all-round consultation.

The school is on a level site in a pleasant side road. It has good sized hard playground and grass areas, with no unusual features except the retention of a number of felled tree trunks which make playground seating and scrambling sites for the children.

The main buildings are single-storey and L-shaped, with the corner of the L occupied by the kitchen and dining hall. Beyond the dining hall in one wing of the L is the assembly hall, and beyond that a two-storey teaching block. The floor of the square hall is five feet lower than that of the dining hall which can therefore be used as a stage and 'green room'; the assembly hall is much used for music and drama and is sound-proofed by a folding partition on the dining hall side and by the interposition of store-rooms on the teaching block side.

In the other wing of the L are first the staff and administrative rooms, next the main entrance and reception area, and finally the second two-storey teaching block. Each block houses the children from two year-groups, one on each floor. Within the area for each year-group are three inter-connecting class bases, each of which can be closed off by partition when desired, and shared working spaces. The details vary with the age-groups; for the younger there are two or three smaller working spaces equipped for clean or messy crafts, for mathematics (which is taught on modern lines using a considerable amount of equipment), for science (which includes facilities for keeping small animals), and for reading with a good supply of books to hand. For the fourth year however there is one single large space with sinks, tiled floor, and working benches at each end, with cookery, needlework and craft equipment adjoining, and with a large open space and easily moveable furniture in the centre. In this room both specialised activities and integrated projects can proceed.

Furniture is crucial. Chairs and tables are lightweight and stackable; many of the storage and working benches are on wheels or castors and are easily moved. Audio-visual apparatus too is either portable by hand or moved on purpose-built trolleys (record players, cassette recorders, filmstrip and slide projectors, radio and television receivers); but in each wing there is one room sound-proofed and fitted with fixed equipment for the showing of films, the use of audio-visual courses in French, and so on.

The choice of furniture and equipment was related to the building, and the combination allows considerable flexibility in teaching approaches, in class, group and individual work, and in the organisation of the school day.

Organisation

The present roll of 380 children in a 3 f.e. school is pleasantly uncrowded, but it is expected to rise. (Nominal accommodation is 420.) In each of the four years there are three classes with a team of four teachers, one of whom holds the post of team leader. As far as he can, the headmaster deploys his staff to give each team a balance of skills—ideally each with one teacher with special skill in language, one in mathematics, one in the arts, and one in a branch of the humanities or science. Naturally with staff changes this is not always possible, but the school has not yet had to face any subject of the curriculum without at least one teacher somewhere on the staff well versed in it and to whom colleagues can refer.

Class teaching is the basic organisation, particularly in the younger groups; but each day the teams make opportunities to bring the children together in different groupings, perhaps for individual or small group work according to interest (in painting, pottery, model-making, needlework, costume, play-writing or acting—all of which may go on at the same time), perhaps in physical education (a variety of games, dance, gymnastics), or perhaps all together to watch and discuss a television programme or to hear a talk from one of the teachers (not necessarily one from the home team). At least one or two sessions weekly are normally devoted to project work, which again is usually planned by the team to encourage co-operation across class boundaries. Though the members of the team are in close daily contact, they nevertheless have planning and review meetings about once a month. The whole staff adopts common practices on many teaching matters, such as handwriting, spelling, mathematical method, and the form of records. There is a general staff meeting before the start of each term, but other brief ones may be arranged to discuss specific matters, whether curricular, social or broadly professional.

Most of the teachers also spend a varying amount of time, according to their personal specialism, working with other years. Individual talents in science, art, drama, music and physical education especially are used in this way, so that most of the teachers combine in their programmes class teaching, membership of a year team, and teaching a special interest. The school also has the services of three part-time teachers, one for French, one for music, and one for remedial education; they cannot be spared for other work.

Staff

The headmaster, a man with twenty years' experience as head or deputy, has spent all his teaching life in primary schools and has been in the forefront locally of educational experiment and advance. A convinced 'Plowden' man, he has had the major voice in the appointment of his staff and it is not surprising therefore that most think as he does and follow his lead.

Approximately one-third of them are experienced teachers from the primary field; most of the others are in their first or second teaching appointment and several are young women teachers recently out of college. One or two members of the staff have had short periods of experience in secondary schools, but this is almost incidental. This school is geared to three principles: the philosophy of primary education explicit in the Plowden Report, team teaching, and concern to help each individual child give of his best. It has proved a good school for young teachers to learn their trade in (few have failed, most have blossomed), and one in which the staff is fired by a common purpose.

Achievement

The headmaster encourages visitors, especially parents. The main foyer gives a foretaste of the school as a whole; it is full of colourful display, paintings, models, photos of recent events, finished products of projects, and—in one large area—book displays with chairs in which adults or children may sit and read. The door of the headmaster's room opens off the foyer; if it is open and he is inside, anyone is free to go in and talk to him; if closed, some-one is inside doing so. Most often, however, the door is open but the headmaster is not inside; he is somewhere around the school, for he believes in knowing every one of his pupils not only by name but also in their educational progress, their family affairs, their health and happiness. In the process of gaining and updating this knowledge he is, needless to say, also in constant contact with his staff and with the detailed work of the school, approving, praising, assessing, questioning, suggesting. This continuous built-in evaluation, which is a main cause of this school's success, is accompanied by a ready smile and a stream of good-humoured and witty comment; maybe the method is not one which would succeed without the backing of a warm personality, but, given that, most teachers are appreciative.

The achievement of the school is remarkable in several ways.

First, learning is made attractive to the great majority of the children; their keen concentration and their ability to work un-aided for long periods, if need be, without a teacher free to advise them, are impressive. Second, they take pleasure in discussing their work and in explaining it to others, and the uninhibited way in which they approach adults or other children for help or simply for comment is significant, for it enables them to form standards of their own and to make their own judgements. Third, they show initiative in seeking out information (one clue to this is the rich store of books the school has built up) and in suggesting new lines of enquiry or new projects to follow. Fourth, the range and quality of the work and activities is surprising—and this needs elaboration. Standards vary, reflecting the native abilities of 380 children; but effort is pretty constant. The result in every branch of the curriculum is some outstanding work, a great deal which most observers would classify as good, and very little which does not show steady improvement, however slow or weak the child. Free writing, both descriptive and imaginative (display spaces, project and individual books are full of it); imaginative painting, pottery, collage and weaving; carefully observed and recorded experiments with soil analysis, plant culture, and crop distribution; accounts of other lands from which some of the children come, together with study of their customs and religious festivals; instrumental and choral music of a high standard; drama and dance, and the opportunity to involve everyone in these corporate activities; learning about the structure of local society and organising entertainments and comforts for the sick, the old, and the handicapped of the neighbourhood; all of these add up to an education colourful, vigorous and varied.

Much of this is not carried out according to set syllabuses. Gearing work to individual children means that much of it is a matter of seizing opportunities which arise unforeseen and which may not be repeated—opportunism in the best sense of the word. This very feature makes it difficult to predict to parents or to the upper school what precise ground the children will cover; but it will be purposeful, and basic skills will be not only acquired but exercised. A recent comment from an upper school head of department visiting Aurora Middle School for the first time was: 'I had no idea of the breadth, the quality and the imagination which I have found in your work here; we shall have to think very hard about this!'

School B *Name:* Victoria Middle School
            Location: Metropolitan District of Irondale
            Age range: 8 to 12
            Roll: 310. In its fifth year as a middle school.

Area served

Part of the inner ring of a large northern industrial city. The housing is tight-packed Victorian terraces, much of it over-crowded and in poor repair; factories, some of them closed, are scattered through the area and there is an almost total lack of play space, apart from one adventure playground which is very popular with younger children at the exploring age and one small park so unimaginatively equipped that simple ball games are the limit of what it can offer. Canals, mainly derelict, present both a fascination and a danger. The education authority has operated a moderately successful play centre in a neighbouring school during two recent summer holiday periods; this is likely to be discontinued as economy measures become more stringent. Many parents are anxious about the way their children spend their spare time, but, since the proportion of working mothers and of shift workers among the fathers is high, it is difficult for them to do much about it. About 10 per cent of the children at Victoria are from overseas, mainly from the Indian sub-continent; many are shy, though most understand English fairly well from their grounding in the First School.

Premises

The Middle and First Schools share the site, which is under size but with no prospect of expansion until the whole area is re-developed at an uncertain but distant date; and it is by no means clear whether a school will then still be needed here. Consequently the Victoria schools are in that unhappy category of being uneconomic to pour money into, the authority very reasonably preferring to build schools on new housing estates where it is certain there will be pupils. As their name implies, the original buildings are Victorian, solid, uncompromising and allowing little scope for remodelling, though the authority's architects have ingeniously inserted smaller rooms at mezzanine level off the staircases of the three-decker building; they serve as staff, medical, and small group teaching rooms. The Middle School occupies, generally speaking, the two upper floors (the arrangement may vary slightly from year to year according to the exact numbers in each of the two schools); it also has a *conversion unit* of prefabricated construction in the playground which gives a further two rooms, one equipped broadly for art and craft activities and the other for domestic subjects, mainly needlecraft, simple dressmaking and cookery. The main building provides a hall and six full-sized classrooms, together with a smaller room used as a library. The classrooms are large and with good display space, though all are short of storage.

The building has three disadvantages difficult to overcome. The first is noise, which echoes along the corridors and off the tiled portions of the walls; and even the conversion unit has to compete for most of the day with outdoor physical education and First School playtimes. The second is that the mezzanine position of the head's, staff and secretary's rooms is withdrawn from the parts of the building where the children are, and that formal arrangements for supervision have therefore to be made; fully informal relations would not be possible even if the staff wished for them. The third is that the enclosed nature of all the classrooms makes integrated, or joint, work involving more than one class difficult (though admittedly not impossible); the difficulty is accentuated by the isolation in the playground of the art and craft domestic subjects, which ideally would have an important part to play in projects or thematic studies.

Organisation

The head's freedom of manoeuvre is restricted by the combination of numbers and accommodation. There is a fair amount of movement in and out of the district, with the result that the number of pupils may vary by 20 or more from term to term, or even within a term. A roll of 310 stretches his resources to the full; with eight full-sized teaching spaces (including the two specially equipped rooms in the conversion unit) and one small group room in which ten or so of the weaker pupils are assembled, all classes except the last have to be between 35 and 39 strong. The hall is fully worked with indoor physical education, music and a little drama; the playground, shared with the First School, is available for about two-thirds of the week. The head battles to keep the library free from use as a class base, reasoning that it is the one place where children can pursue some individual enquiry. In order to give each class some use of the hall, art and craft, and domestic subjects rooms, precise time-tabling is necessary; even so, it is not easy always to time-table for the customary half rather than full classes in the two special rooms, since it is virtually only the hall (and the playground in fine weather) which provides space for the other half. It is possible to show films and to use the school television set in two of the large classrooms, but the operation necessitates classes changing over and this is not popular.

It is no surprise to find therefore that the basis of the organisation is work in single classes, except where they divide to use the special rooms. There is no question of planning, as Aurora was able to do, for a year-group as a whole, or to allow groups within the year to form and reform for different purposes during the day. There is also virtually no chance for individual children to leave their base and pursue enquiries elsewhere, except in the library (there is an unwritten understanding that if a child goes to the library and finds it full, he returns to his own room). Apart from the exigencies of time-tabling so far mentioned, the head has no objection to teachers planning and working a project jointly or to exchanging classes for a particular purpose, provided that he knows what is afoot; and to some extent this happens, as of course it did in many junior schools well before their transformation into 8 to 12 middle schools.

Throughout the four-year course most subjects are taught in most classes by the class teacher, but there are some exceptions. Eight of the establishment of $11\frac{1}{2}$ teachers are class teachers in this sense, while the ninth works for rather more than half her time with the small remedial group and for the remainder takes classes in drama. Of the remaining teachers, one does further remedial work with small groups withdrawn from other classes (they include a number of the children from overseas who need additional help with their English), one divides his time between music and physical education, and the third comes in half-time for domestic subjects, mainly simple cookery and needlecraft. The last two are the only members of the staff who have trained specially for these subjects; the others are all general primary teachers by both training and experience.

The curricular cover varies in its strengths and weaknesses from year to year, for there is a considerable staff turnover and incoming teachers do not always match exactly the skills of those who have left. At present science and handicraft are poorly provided for, there being no teacher with special knowledge of either. There is no real leader in art, and French has occurred only sporadically; the head is now convinced that in his situation it is unrealistic to attempt it, with no continuity of teacher, no suitable room, and very little possibility of forming teaching groups small enough for the oral methods favoured to-day. The basic subjects of English, mathematics (in which the head himself gives something of a lead) and social studies are thoroughly dealt with on a class teacher basis. The head insists on careful records of the progress of individual children and makes regular use of standardised tests in reading and mathematics, so that here at least the staff feel their objective to be clear. Drama, music and domestic subjects are well taught within the limit of time and facilities.

Staff

The head is pragmatic and down to earth in his outlook and leadership. After many years of struggle against overcrowding, problems induced by a high measure of social deprivation in the area, high turnover of staff, and much backwardness among his pupils, he could perhaps hardly survive were he not. A man of energy, drive, plain speech, and an eye for immediate detail rather than a long-term Utopia, he stands on his own feet and expects others to do the same. Nearly half his staff, like himself, are in their fifties; they competently hold the line as they have done for twenty years, but they have little time for innovation or research and are unlikely to change. Of the younger teachers, two are in their early thirties, hard-working, infusing some sparkle into the music and physical education in particular; they are hoping for promotion and if successful will leave a gap not easily filled. The other four full-time teachers, three women and a man, are in their first post; two are frankly struggling and unlikely to stay, for the brusque matter-of-fact approach of the head, while effective with the tougher young teachers, seems to the weaker ones unsympathetic and gives them little help. The half-time domestic subjects teacher is an older married woman with a background of former secondary school teaching; she is well able to command the interest of the girls though her natural tendency is to work at her own subject in isolation.

All these teachers are hard-working and concerned for the children of the neighbourhood; many give a lot of unobtrusive help to individuals after school hours and take considerable trouble to try to make parents understand their children's difficulties. They are not in the forefront of curricular experiment, and both the social setting of the school and the restrictions of its premises lead—almost compel—them to pursue an 'everyone for himself' policy, in which co-operative teaching or joint projects can find little room.

Achievement

As a community, the school is tightly organised, firmly driven (rather than led), practically minded, lacking the finer shades in its human relationships—but stable; and in the grey belt of the inner city stability is a quality not to be under-valued. It is perhaps better for the tough-skinned rather than the thin-skinned, for the extrovert rather than the quiet or timid, for the locally born rather than the new arrival. It offers something established by long tradition, familiar, to many reassuring; but to others it has an air, however faint, of Wordsworth's shades of the prison-house.

The staff are determined that no pupil, so far as they can ensure, shall move on to the upper school without an adequate mastery of the basic subjects and skills. They strive to inculcate —and in the main succeed—an orderly fashion of work and an ability to follow instructions. The language and literature are practical rather than imaginative—though some brisk simple drama may be seen. Its art, in the main, is limp and does little to illuminate, say, history, the study of other lands, religious or poetical experiences (which are not frequent in most classes anyway). How much of an understanding of the structures of society and of the amalgam of qualities and influences which make people what they are penetrates to the majority of the pupils is doubtful; but the staff might well say that one does not study finer emotional and social points when the first call is for the skills essential to survival. The children's work is sound, solid, mainly uninspired; much of it is fragmented and seems to consist of little self-contained packets the relevance of which to what happened an hour earlier or an hour later often cannot be determined.

This is a school with many good qualities. Thirty years ago it would unhesitatingly have been recognised as a good junior school. But the world changes; society changes, and with it human relations and the sum of human knowledge change. Thirty years ago, and much more recently than that, the Middle School was not even an idea; now it is a reality, a new educational institution. How far can a school be an example of a new institution if it is not susceptible to new ideas? We return to this question in Chapter 7, after looking at some further examples of to-day's middle schools.

These first two schools have both been working with the age range of 8 to 12 years; the next three composite examples deal with the 9 to 13 age range, and the differences between the two, as was indicated in Chapter 5, may be considerable. The 9 to 13 schools are generally larger; their needs for specialist teaching accommodation are greater; their antecedents in an area or in a particular school may be primary, or secondary, or a combination of both; and they have the opportunity to make a real bridge between the two differing concepts of education. In many areas a great deal of thought and planning preceded their introduction, with results of which these next examples are typical.

School C *Name:*   Meadowvale Middle School
             Location: Greenstead, County of Bankshire
             Age range: 9 to 13
             Roll: 540 pupils. In its fifth year as a middle
                            school.

Area served

Greenstead is an ancient market town which in the last fifty
years has attracted a little light industry and, most recently, has
greatly expanded as a residential area serving two or three much
larger towns within a 25 mile radius—the coming of a nearby
motorway in particular having accelerated the process. It is
prosperous, with only a few small local pockets of poverty or
bad housing. Three middle schools feed pupils to the single

comprehensive upper school, which Meadowvale Middle School adjoins. Meadowvale is itself housed in adapted and extended buildings which were formerly a secondary modern school.

Premises

The site is spacious, having been first reserved for educational use under the earlier generous requirements prescribed by the statutory regulations of 1948, long since superseded. There is room for a pleasant lay-out of trees, flower beds, and small pools in front of the buildings, and for a large plot of land adjoining the separate rural science building which is shared with the upper school; this plot is of course used for practical work in connection with the rural science course which it is natural to find in what is still a country market town. The original secondary modern buildings were in the traditional style of the early 1950s, consisting mainly of straightforward classrooms, laboratories and other specialist rooms; additional rooms were added to cope with a 'bulge' of pupils in the 1960s. Meadowvale is itself still catering for a 'bulge'; although designated a four-form entry school (ie one admitting four classes of 30 to 35 pupils each year), it has in fact an additional form in each of the two upper years, thus raising the number of pupils from the intended 480 to its present 540. Two mobile classrooms on the site enable the school to accommodate the 'bulge', which is not expected to recur.

Remodelling the former secondary buildings has given more flexibility than the original design could possibly have allowed. Walls between classrooms and corridors have been removed, in whole or in part, thus increasing the effective working and display space; and in some parts of the school former cloakrooms opening off corridors have been similarly converted to working use, being replaced elsewhere by new cloakrooms requiring less space. Despite initial fears, the passage of people through these spaces rarely seems to disturb the pupils working there. The former specialist rooms have been retained for the most part, though newly equipped with moveable furniture instead of fixed benches and with provision of some small working bays instead of leaving the whole large room open for class teaching. There is thus excellent accommodation for science, handicraft (wood and simple metalwork), art (a large studio equipped for pottery at one end), light crafts, domestic subjects, including a needlecraft and design room which has direct access to the art studio through a folding partition, and physical education which has inherited the gymnasium and in the summer also has the use of an outdoor swimming pool in addition to the games pitches. A former general purposes room has been fitted up as the library, and the insertion of a soundproof partition into a suitably placed classroom has provided two music practice rooms. A final spare classroom has been turned into a drama studio. The school is well equipped with audio-visual apparatus, mainly lightweight and easily portable. Most of the classrooms and their adjoining display spaces are allocated to particular subjects, though as they have to serve also as form bases there is often a sharing of the display space with class or group project work which is going on in the particular year.

The school is perhaps fortunate in that the education authority was able and willing to allocate sufficient funds for re-modelling on this scale. The imaginative use of space previously unused for teaching purposes, and the relatively inexpensive re-equipping of specialist rooms, combine to produce a remarkably successful conversion. At the design stage the architect's department worked in conjunction with the headmaster designate and a consultative panel.

Organisation and Curriculum

In these closely linked fields are implemented the aims of the school as enunciated by the head and applied by the staff. In the months preceding the opening of the school there was systematic consultation among those appointed to it, and the process has become an integral part of school life. The staff define their task as helping their pupils through the transition from childhood to adolescence which is implicit in the 9 to 13 age range, and doing so by moving gradually from a relatively unstructured learning situation in the early years to a much more organised, though still flexible, approach as the child matures and his manner of thinking and learning becomes more systematic. The changes in organisation from year to year, as he moves up the school, reflect this. Basic practice is that at all stages the pupil shall have opportunity to move freely from one resource area to another as his assignment requires, to suggest to his teacher the methods of working and lines of enquiry he would like to pursue, and, as he matures, to follow some of these studies in depth over a period of some days. At the beginning of each day he consults his form teacher about his programme, and at the end of the day he reports on what he has done. Freedom is not for the pupil alone; the teacher too, who is involved very directly in all this, is free to organise groups, to influence assignments within his class (for some purposes more widely), and to consult his colleagues on areas of the curriculum where they are more knowledgeable than he.

Within this framework, staff undertake three major rôles. In each of the first and second years there are four forms (which would be known as 'classes' in most primary schools but are generally called 'forms' in secondary schools; in middle schools either usage may be found)—and five each in the two upper 'bulge' years. The form teacher is responsible for the personal progress of the pupils in his form, and, as mentioned above, acts as director of each pupil's studies day by day. He does not work in isolation, however; in each year an experienced member of staff is appointed year leader, and his task is to ensure that the ground covered in each form, though not following a common syllabus (of which there are none) is broadly similar insofar as the development of skills, working approaches, and social experience is concerned. He co-ordinates the work of his team of form teachers and of those who teach special subjects within his year; he suggests or assists with team teaching and joint projects, and keeps himself aware of children who are underperforming, having learning difficulties, and so on. It is he who calls for advice from the remedial teachers or who decides whether a child should be moved into another form, should there appear to be any personality clash or lack of sympathy between a form teacher and the child. There are, incidentally, no separate remedial forms in the school; learning or personality problems are dealt with on an individual basis without taking the child outside his year to do so, and the organisation already outlined is well suited to the formation of small groups for remedial work for short periods of time. The help of the two remedial teachers on the staff is much invoked in this way.

The third rôle taken by members of staff is that of consultant or of specialist teacher. Except for some part-timers, there are very few teachers who teach exclusively one subject; but there are teachers with special training or special knowledge in every subject of the curriculum. The senior among them, known as consultants, are not only what their title implies (and every teacher is free to, and is expected to, call upon them as needed), but in addition they naturally spend a large part of their time teaching their own subject and co-ordinating the work of other, less well informed teachers of it. Art, music, science, handicraft, domestic subjects, rural science, and physical education are handled especially in this way; but consultants are not confined to them. Though every form teacher is likely to be taking some English with his own form, this does not exclude the need for a well qualified consultant English teacher, probably a graduate in English and one who devotes much time to keeping in touch with new publications, experiments, and developments generally; he is not only available for consultation but from time to time he calls a meeting of all those teaching English to familiarise them with the latest developments, to introduce new stock purchased (books, films, tapes, records), to arrange visits to theatres, exhibitions, and so on—or just to have a 'trouble-shooting' session in which all unburden themselves freely. And what is true to English applies equally to mathematics, social studies, religious education—in fact, to most of the curriculum.

The key people in these curricular and organisational patterns are therefore the year leaders and the consultants; each leads a team, in the first case of form teachers and in the second of subject teachers. There is of course a good deal of interlocking; all form teachers are teaching subjects, and all subject teachers are contributing to the work within the years. Contact is partly on an informal day-to-day basis and partly by more formal meetings or procedures at particular times. Year teams meet weekly at a time when the music teachers are leading a general hymn practice, and the four year leaders meet with the head and his two deputies, to discuss pastoral as well as curricular matters, weekly during a lunch hour. The head is a firm believer in prevention being better than cure, and the early exchange of information about children whose behaviour or whose progress appears to cause concern often enables help to be given before major difficulties have developed. Consultants call their meetings as required, and this may vary a great deal between, for instance, subjects involving many teachers such as English and mathematics and those involving only one or two such as needlecraft and French.

In the first two years the team of form teachers undertakes most of the work except the French and music in both years and, additionally, science in the second year. (One of the second year teachers is a very interested musician and he joins in the music; it is the head's aim that individual talents shall be welcomed and given scope in this way.) In the third year specialist teaching increases, with all pupils spending some time at handicraft, domestic subjects, rural science, and a choice of activities in music and art. Some special courses are organised for particular groups of pupils—especially for those with learning difficulties, whether of speech, reading, manual skills or difficulties of social adjustment, and for very talented pupils who are capable of a faster pace and a wider range of interest than their fellows. In the final year these arrangements continue but are intensified, so that around three-quarters of the working week is in the hands of specialist subject teachers and there is more emphasis on systematic and sequential working and on such matters as lay-out and presentation of work.

Neither the head nor his two deputies (one a man and one a woman) have given up actual teaching, though outside calls (from visitors, colleges of education, local organisations, the education office) make it unwise for the head to commit himself to a definite time-table; but when not so tied down he is constantly around the school, observing, talking, appraising, encouraging. Both deputies teach in specialist departments despite heavy administration loads, among which relations with parents, the frequent scrutiny of individual records of children's progress, and liaison with both the upper school and the contributory first schools figure largely. Their attitudes and influence are pervasive, and the care they take with young teachers especially is a rewarding investment for the future.

In a school of this size records are very important. The head's policy is to allow each teacher to keep records in his own preferred form (and some are ingenious in the use of hieroglyphs and other shorthand forms!) so long as he can produce and interpret them at any time to his year leader or deputies. Towards the end of each term however a school pro-forma has to be completed in respect of each pupil, to which several teachers may contribute, thus building up a profile of personality and progress. This regular record includes performance in standardised tests of ability and attainment, and a reference to other sources such as a child guidance report which would not necessarily be made available to all teachers.

Staff

Numerically, the staffing looks generous; in fact it is none too much for what the school is doing. The heaviest demands on staff time arise first from the freedom of pupils to pursue their own enquiries to a considerable extent, which naturally generates a demand on their part for a great deal of individual consultation, and secondly from the need for a good number of teachers able to direct specialist courses and to supervise well equipped specialist rooms and apparatus. With 26 full-time teachers (excluding the head) and four part-timers whose service is equivalent to another two full-timers, the ratio against 540 pupils is slightly more generous than 1 to 20. With fewer teachers, the school would have to attempt less; as it is, it is able to aim at the target of what its senior members believe a middle school should be.

When the school opened five years ago, the head and approximately half his staff came from the former secondary modern school which Meadowvale replaced. The remainder were equally divided between teachers from primary schools and beginners fresh from colleges of education. The appointments to senior posts held a rough balance between primary and secondary experience; one of the deputy heads, the first and second year leaders, and the consultant teachers in English and religious education came from the primary field. Since the opening, the staff has increased by five to its present number (the school did not open at full strength, and the 'bulge' has also necessitated additional appointments.) There has been some movement out, partly of senior members on promotion and partly through marriage of young women members of staff. Almost all the resultant new appointments (the senior vacancies having all been filled from within) have been of beginners direct from college; the field has been good at this level and many of those appointed have followed a four-year course and hold a B.Ed. degree. All those appointed have wished to teach in middle schools and have brought real enthusiasm to their work. The strength of the field has enabled the head to make appointments which give the right curricular balance, so that the school is now very well staffed indeed for its task. The feature which has occasioned some concern is the almost total lack of applications from experienced teachers from outside the school for advertised senior posts; this phenomenon is one noted by other lively and experimentally inclined middle schools elsewhere, and its cause is not clear. If it persists, the consequences could eventually be unfortunate, since knowledge of good and successful practice spreads most easily when its exponents take it with them to fresh fields.

Though the school does little in the way of formal in-service training for its own staff, it could be said that the consultant system, allied to the friendly relations and the general enthusiasm of the Meadowvale teachers, provides the best form of further training, especially for the new young members of staff. The head encourages attendance at courses and workshops, but the take-up is small since there is as yet only an inadequately provided Teachers' Centre in the town which has not yet really got under way. Some of the senior members of staff have however attended courses at the county education authority's residential teachers' centre and have found them beneficial.

The authority has been helpful over ancillary staff. A qualified secretary and two general office assistants are able to give appreciable clerical help to most senior post holders, and in addition a clerical assistant divides her time between the library and the adjoining resources centre. Two members of the teaching staff, English and science specialists respectively, are responsible for the direction of these two collections, but the detailed help of the assistant greatly economises their time. A team of technicians serves all three of the middle schools in the town and in part the upper school too; Meadowvale's share amounts to the equivalent of one and a half full-time technicians, who maintain and service the equipment in the science, handicraft, rural science and visual aids departments—and who, since relations are good, will at time go beyond this if needed.

Achievement

The head defined the school's objectives, before it opened, as producing happy and well adjusted children with a positive and lively attitude towards their work and the community, skilled in using investigational approaches, good at self-learning, and whose actual educational attainment matches their potential. This definition reflects much of the philosophy of primary education enunciated with approval in the Plowden Report. In particular it implies children who can work for long periods on their own, but who also know how to ask adults for help and who can equally work with groups of their fellows. It implies that how they learn is more important than what they learn, at least in the earlier stages. And from this it implies that much of their work will cross subject barriers, that much of it will consist of projects in which knowledge from various subjects is brought together (for instance, a local study will inevitably draw upon history, geography, current affairs, statistics, maybe literature, and will need for presentation of its findings the skill of the writer, modeller, illustrator, and so on), and that different pupils, though nominally in the same form, will cover different ground. It is an educational process encouraging the pupil to be himself, think for himself, and to roam widely enough through fields of knowledge to discover where his talents really lie— whether he is a writer, a scientific observer, a mathematician, a musician, a painter, or one who is happiest wielding tools indoors or out.

But the declared aim of the school is also to help pupils make successfully the transition to more adult modes of learning and to acquire generally agreed components of knowledge within the principal areas of study. They have to graduate to the more controlled assignments and the more structured disciplines which ought to precede transfer to the upper school. Music is no longer just making joyful individual sounds on easy instruments; it requires sustained effort on a well recognised instrument and perhaps then the ability to work precisely as a member of a band or an orchestra (the school has two) under a conductor. Art is no longer simply splashing paint spontaneously on to paper or canvas; there are techniques to be mastered and the properties of materials, tools and fabrics to be learned. Mutatis mutandis, appropriate disciplines will be found in every subject or aspect of learning.

Achievement by these criteria is extremely good. Pupils are busy, occupied, well disciplined, friendly and co-operative. The actual quality of the finished work in every year and in every field impresses; what the ablest pupils have produced would not disgrace the higher forms of many an upper school, and freshness and spontaneity do match pride in performance. Such things as the great murals in the foyer, the pottery in the showcase in front of them, the polished wooden bowls, stools, shields and the like in the showcase opposite, tell of variety, quality, and of children achieving their potential. The performances from the actors, the stage hands, the chorus, the dancers, and the orchestra when the school performs its annual play (which it has written, costumed and arranged, engaging the efforts of literally hundreds of pupils in all) simply match these in different fields. And in the more formal skills of reading, writing, and calculating the same will be found true—though the short stories, the original poetry, and the mathematical-cum-scientific projections go well beyond what used to be known as the three Rs. (To quote one example—have you ever tried to design a house for which clay, wattle and thatch are the only permitted materials and in which the only permitted shapes are triangles? the mathematics is interesting and calls for prior investigation of the properties of the materials and for precise thinking about the best use to be made of them.)

Of course there are failures; of course there are problems which the staff will frankly discuss with any sympathetic listener. How does one persist with the child who seems interested in nothing? Is the approach to remedial work sufficiently strong in continuity? How can the domestic subjects be better related to other branches of the curriculum? Ought there not to be some formal study of history and geography before the children leave? and if so, how should the selection be made? All of these questions are in the minds of head and staff. But there is no doubt that for the 12- and 13-year-old children in this school the range of their interests and work has been widened, that they are learning how to make choices and decisions, are well grounded in the essential skills, and have an enthusiasm for learning which often they had lost by this age in time past.

The head attributes the success to careful planning, continual discussion about both individual children and the curriculum, to the buildings and facilities provided, and most of all to the attitudes of the staff. With this he couples the importance of the daily school assemblies; the school does not meet entire every day, but on at least one day in the week assembles in much smaller units. All assemblies are first and foremost corporate occasions, relaxed, friendly, concerned with people in the school, the town, and more widely; but the head stresses also the importance of the element of well prepared worship as something which introduces children to a dimension higher than themselves. Their own work contributes to this, through their art, music, drama, dance, and simple reading and singing. In a time when assemblies are under question in some quarters, in this school at any rate their value and relevance are undoubted.

If at Meadowvale we see a school with almost everything in its favour, we see too the achievement of which, given such conditions, the middle school is capable—very good indeed!

School D *Name:*   Millrace Middle School
           Location: Metropolitan District of Carborough
           Age range: 9 to 13
           Roll: 640. In its fourth year.

Area served

This is a new school, designed and built to serve the population
from a major new housing programme on the outskirts of a large
industrial town, linked to the development of nearby industrial
estates; but some of the residents travel to work in the town
centre or elsewhere. There was a small amount of private
housing of modest though good quality in the area before the
recent expansion; most of the new housing, though not all, is in
the form of Council estates. Both area and school therefore are

new. Much effort went into establishing contact with the residents from the start, and relations generally are good.

Premises

The school is purpose built as a 5 form entry middle school. This education authority, unlike many, saw the middle school as having strong affinities with, and certainly accustoming its pupils to, secondary school practices and the design reflects this belief. Specialist teaching was envisaged and generous accommodation for it is a key feature of the design. It is however no pale copy of the secondary schools of the past; it incorporates many features which make for flexibility in working and which show an understanding of the characteristics of children in these middle years.

The land was sloping and the contours have been well used, both to give interest to the outdoor parts of the site and to relate the different heights of parts of the buildings pleasantly to each other. Hall, dining room and gymnasium follow secondary school models, though all three are squarer than used to be customary; this is not only acoustically better but makes it easier to mount arena-type drama productions in the hall and to supervise a variety of gymnastic activities at the same time in the gymnasium. The rest of the building, which is on two floors, consists basically of four nearly square wings built out from the corners of a hollow square formed by the hall, gymnasium, dining room and kitchens, library, and administrative and staff rooms. The upper floor is broadly given over to classrooms, the lower to specialist subject rooms. The design is ingenious in its detail, and no square foot appears to have been wasted. There is a basic assumption that corridors and other separate circulation space are wasteful, and that pupils and staff can move through teaching accommodation as they need to without disrupting what is going on. In practice this proves to be true—partly, as will be seen, because there is fairly tight time-tabling and not a lot of movement except at specified change-over times.

On the classroom floor, each wing contains four classrooms, with a central working space between the first two; this space is differently equipped in each of the wings, but all include some provision for consulting books and for quiet working in small groups on, say, maps, charts, drawings, plans, and designs which may vary from a town planning exercise to dress design. The two end classrooms are unusually large (over 1,000 square feet, or the former standard size for a secondary school laboratory or practical room). They have water, sinks, and some fixed bench provision against the walls which enables them to be fitted out simply for practical work in mathematics, environmental studies, and some forms of art and craft—and which can just as simply be varied from term to term. Each wing is intended on this floor to provide class bases for a full year's pupils; and since, generally speaking, one of the five classes in each year is always out of the wing engaged on some specialist work, this operates smoothly, though clearly requiring careful timetabling.

On the ground floor are specialist rooms—science laboratories, art and craft studios, domestic science and handicraft rooms, rooms equipped with audio-visual aids for the use of films, television, and the audio-visual courses now widely used in the teaching of foreign languages, plus a music room to supplement the use made of the hall. Here too are two rooms used for work with groups of children suffering from backwardness or learning difficulties—sensitively furnished with comfortable chairs, carpeted, and generally given a homely and bright look. The school has shown some ingenuity in the use made of spaces originally designed for storage; one such, for instance, between two science laboratories has been fitted out as an animal room, where rabbits, guinea pigs, hamsters (the actual species vary from time to time) are kept and studied.

An imaginative touch is the use of the entrance foyer, which is unusually large. In addition to plants and displays of some aspects of the school's current work, part of it is screened off as a discussion-cum-waiting room where parents, students, and other visitors can find a place to sit and talk (often not easily done in a full and busy school). No doubt this facility has helped to encourage parents to visit the school and to feel welcome in it.

The inner courtyard houses plants and flower beds and a number of seats; it not only looks attractive but in mild weather offers pleasant relaxation during the lunch hour for pupils who do not wish to be vigorously active. Seats, either made in the woodwork room from donated or cheaply acquired material or actual gifts to the school, are also a feature of the grounds, where they are dotted around both in the flower gardens at the front and on the sunny side of the building; a nice touch is to find one reserved for staff! The value of the garden is more than just visual; several of the flower beds are being used experimentally to investigate the effect of soil, climate and fertilisers on strains of plants, and there are also two pools in which aquatic plants and creatures are being studied.

This school is well-designed and compact, pleasant to work and learn in. It combines excellent features both old and new. It is in effect geared to particular organisational and teaching approaches, to which we now turn.

Organisation and Curriculum

The general pattern of school organisation owes more to traditional secondary than to primary practice. The class is the normal teaching unit, and class sizes average 30 pupils. (In addition to the basic 20 classes, there are two small remedial groups of around 10 to 15 pupils each, though for many activities they join their year group.) The school day is firmly time-tabled with eight teaching periods half an hour long, though there is a good deal of working in 'double' periods of a full hour. This permits reasonable flexibility; for English or science, for instance, most teachers would wish to have an hour at their disposal, whereas for French, for gymnastics or dance, or for the showing of a teaching or television film, the half-hour is a more appropriate unit. There cannot, however, be much of the individual research and enquiry undertaken by pupils in their own time and at their own pace which we have seen in two of the other schools under review. (This is not to say that individual enquiry does not take place—only that it has to be organised in a different way.)

A break of five minutes is reckoned between periods, simply to allow those who have to move to do so without rushing; but classes at work in a 'double' period do not stop. Each school day opens with an assembly, followed by a fifteen minute period when each class is with its class teacher who checks on individual programmes, studies comments about his pupils' progress from other teachers, or answers any questions which pupils themselves have to raise.

The basis of the teaching is specialism, but to a varying degree according to the age of the children and the interests of the teacher. Certainly in the first two years each class is taken by its own teacher for 40 to 50 per cent of its time, and he will therefore be teaching a block of subjects, not just a single one. For the rest of his time he will be employing his own specialism with other classes. Approximately one-third of the staff do not look after a class, but are full-time specialists, though this should not be too narrowly interpreted. For instance, to specialise in science in this middle school involves elements of land utilisation, soil and crop study, meteorology, plant and animal life, and at times astronomy and cosmology in addition to the more well-worn paths of science teaching; while among the aspects of art and craft met by pupils during their four-year course are painting, collage, fabric and potato printing, tie dyeing, modelling in clay, chalk and soap, pottery and even origami—so there is no necessity for anyone's specialism to become narrow. In the third and fourth years the amount of specialist teaching in pupils' time-tables increases, one of the school's aims being to have prepared their pupils for an easy transition to the likely way of life they will encounter in the upper school.

Though the head has sought staff with specialist knowledge and interests, his intention was not to set up an institution so specialist that the relation to each other of different fields of knowledge was overlooked. Consequently, though there are specialist teachers, there are no 'departments' and no heads of departments. The key people are the four year co-ordinators, who exercise general oversight over the whole of the time-tables and teaching programmes within their year and who ensure that teachers concerned with classes in their year do talk to each other and do, where they can, relate their programmes to each other. They call 'year meetings' as they think fit, see and discuss all schemes of work, and supervise all records. A good part of their own teaching, whatever their specialism, is to classes within their own year. Naturally enough, in each specialism one teacher is designated to be responsible for the laboratory, workshop or studio concerned, for stock and for planning ahead, and equally naturally other teachers in the same field talk to each other and to him. Requests for new stock, books, equipment and so on are considered annually by the head and year co-ordinators in conference; the usual result is that the head picks out special priorities and apportions the remainder of the available money among the various claimants, who decide on the detail of what they wish to buy; the whole operation is overseen by the deputy head.

The curriculum is seen in five main blocks, which to some extent cut across traditional secondary subject boundaries and approach the common primary outlook. They are the humanities (the study of man and his achievements, incorporating language, literature, history, and the arts), environmental studies, science, mathematics, and physical education including dance and drama. The staff have not found it easy to fit either religious education or French into this framework, and these two subjects are time-tabled separately, even if logic would have placed them within the humanities. In practice it is also found that art and craft, domestic subjects, and handicraft (wood and metalwork) need additional specialist time-tabling, the amount increasing as the pupils move up from year to year. The different areas are useful as a guide for planning and for the drawing up of sylla-buses in particular, ensuring that work is not fragmented and that, for instance, a study of a historical period will bring in the literature, the scientific discovery, and the features of its artistic and musical life as well as the simple 'history'. Team teaching is rarely used, but related teaching is frequent.

Two other features are of interest. All classes are mixed ability groups; but in the third and fourth years the school finds it better to 'set' (ie to re-group pupils according to their actual level of attainment) throughout the year in mathematics; they feel the gap in attainment between the ablest and the slowest is too great for mixed ability classes to be fair to either. Whether French should be similarly treated is under consideration. The second feature is that at certain times during the week very able pupils are withdrawn from their classes for some very exacting work in small groups to give them the kind of intellectual challenge which they need to fulfil their potential; in a way, this is the equivalent of taking out the backward or those with learning difficulties for special attention, as is done in the two remedial groups, and it is to be commended.

Staff

The establishment is for the head and 28 full-time staff, giving a pupil-teacher ratio (excluding the head, as is customary in such calculations) of 23 to 1. Of these 20 act as class teachers, four being year co-ordinators. There are seven other full-timers and three part-timers (the school gains a little on the strict establishment, since the part-timers each come in for approximately half the week, for French, music and art respectively). The seven are the deputy head (a woman), the senior master who is also an English specialist, and other specialists in remedial education, science, wood and metalwork, domestic subjects, and art and design, the last-named teacher working with girls at both the skills of dressmaking and the design and decorative aspects of needlework. The staff is well balanced to cover all the curricular areas, any shortages in the four years of its life having been temporary and brief. The staff has also been stable, with remarkably little movement out and in; though there is always an element of chance in this, serving staff clearly find it congenial and advertised posts have all attracted good fields. Among the features which account for this are probably the new and purpose-built premises and the clear, firm direction and organisation which allows teachers in the main to concentrate on what they feel they can do best.

Around half the staff are graduates or equivalent, mainly in their specialism with an additional year of professional training. The remainder, except for two or three older and very experienced teachers who qualified in the days of two-year training courses, are from three year college of education courses with subsequent teaching experience of between one and ten years. The graduates had mainly taught in secondary schools; several but not all of the college of education trained teachers had primary experience. The head himself, though he had never taught in a primary school, had long been deeply interested in developments there and is moreover very abreast of thought and research in child development and in educational psychology; his secondary experience too had been both wide and practical, including lately responsibility for a secondary modern school where he was able closely to observe the charac- teristics of the 11 to 13 year old pupils and the problems they faced on transition from their primary schools. The deputy head- mistress was formerly head of a primary school; the combina- tion, both of experience and personalities, has proved admirable for giving confidence and clear leadership to this middle school in its early years. With the year co-ordinators, whom they meet weekly, they form a kind of 'cabinet', where both short and long term decisions are taken—the last word always resting with the head. Both the head and deputy insist on teaching not less than one-third of the week, a fact which undoubtedly helps them always to have their finger accurately on the pulse of the school and to recognise any change in its moods.

The ancillary support is adequate and efficient; among the most valuable members are the full-time library assistant, who works in conjunction with one of the English specialists, and two technicians responsible for maintenance of teaching equip- ment and for constructing apparatus as called upon by the teaching staff. In this school all members of the ancillary staff are members of the staff room and feel that they have a real stake in the health and progress of the school.

The school is much used by teacher training establish- ments for student observation and practice; students, tutors and other professional visitors are welcomed and drawn upon for help.

Achievement

There is nothing tentative about Millrace Middle School. Some observers would describe it as another school which has everything in its favour; but this would be an over-simplification. Certainly the buildings are attractive and functionally effective; but the organisation is well matched to them and enormous trouble is taken with the complexities of time-tabling to ensure that the best results are extracted from it. Both staff and pupils go about their work purposefully and much work of high quality results; but this would not be achieved without clearly thought out aims and objectives and careful appraisal of work done. It is a school free of major disciplinary troubles and which has an excellent attendance record; but this is surely connected with skilful and lively teaching from well-informed teachers which interests the pupils and makes demands on them. If there is little 'integrated' work, of the kind possible in schools of a more open-plan design, there is a wide range of work within each subject or curricular field here, both theoretical and practical, and related to other subjects by teachers who are themselves conscious of the unity of human knowledge. The actual levels of performance attained by the best pupils in literature, in mathematics, in some branches of science and art, and in the domestic and workshop subjects, certainly surpass what is customarily found from twelve and thirteen year old pupils in most secondary schools; but what is equally important is that slower pupils seem in no way discouraged by this but themselves gain satisfaction from turning out the best of which they are capable. The attitude towards 'remedial' work typified by locating it in two of the most attractively furnished rooms in the school not unnaturally gives confidence to those pupils who spend part of their time there; but this would not be achieved without genuine sympathy and understanding on the part of the staff, and the back-up of well chosen and up-to-date books and equipment for learning. In a school where the working objectives are clear, where work is made interesting and there is pride in presentation, on the part of both staff and children, it is not surprising that relations all round are good. It is a happy school because it is a busy school; and busy to some purpose, because the leadership is firm and definite and because planning, whether of a four-year course in broad outline or of next week's work in detail, is thorough, careful, and backed up by an exact choice of books, equipment and materials and precise arrangements for the use of necessary rooms and facilities.

The head has been fortunate in appointing staff to whom this framework and method of working is congenial; but the credit is due to him for knowing exactly what kind of people he wanted, perhaps best summed up by saying that he required evidence on both their attitudes and their actual professional knowledge; vagueness and improvisation are not the right formulae for fitting into this school. One or two teachers of this kind fairly soon left, and it was better so; for, however successful they might be in different surroundings, Millrace is characterised by a perceptible unity of purpose and approach which does not, however, stop individual teachers exerting their own individualism within these bounds.

The school is highly thought of locally. In a not very articulate area, the number of parents who will visit the school informally as well as for functions is high and growing. They have direct access to the teacher they wish to see, though they are asked to come at times likely to be convenient or to send an advance message if they cannot. The head and his deputy try to know as many as possible, and have no reservations about visiting homes themselves when this seems the best way of making contact; they expect other, especially younger, teachers to consult them first before they do the same. This positive attitude, friendly and firm, must have done something to give stability to the life of the large new community in the area served by the school.

The school also makes a valuable contribution to liaison with other schools. As the largest of the middle schools serving the local comprehensive upper school, the head has been able to take the lead in promoting effective liaison; the upper school head, appointed around the same time to an equally new school, was like-minded and Millrace in the early stages played host to a number of conferences and meetings which got detailed liaison under way. The contributory first schools are not forgotten; the head or his deputy visit each for a working lunch once a term, and during the summer term there is more direct contact on the part of staff working in the first year. The continuity of the educational process is in fact understood—another reason, perhaps, why the staff can be proud of the part which, as a middle school, Millrace plays in the process.

School E   *Name:*   St. Wulstan's Church of England
                               Middle School
               Location: Underdown, County of Homeshire
               Age range: 9 to 13
               Roll: 360. In its fourth year.

Area served

Underdown is one of the many former small towns of considerable antiquity in the Home Counties which have greatly increased
in size since the war as pleasant dormitory areas. Most of its
working population work away from Underdown, in central
London to which there is a good rail service or in offices or on
factory estates in a nearby 'New Town' or elsewhere within a

radius of 20 miles or so. Though largely a dormitory area, this
does not mean that there is no community sense; there was
already something of an established social and cultural life to
build on, and many of the new residents lend their support to
efforts to develop or strengthen local activities; in this the
schools play no mean part through parent-teacher associations
and through further education and leisure pursuits for young
people and adults in the evenings. There is not much sub-
standard housing and deprivation, in the sense in which it is
found in the inner city areas, hardly exists. This is not to say
that there are no social problems; pressures of family relationships, finance, the executive rat race, and others, bear upon
many of the families and can prey upon the minds of children
the more because many of them are of the kind which families
conceal from outsiders at all costs. Most of the children are
however approachable and articulate, and many of the parents
are keen to help the school.

As a voluntary (in this case Church of England) school, the
Governors have some control over the admissions; in particular,
parents who are members of the Church of England and who
live within a reasonable distance from the school may be
accorded priority. Not only do pupils come to the school from
all parts of the town, but many also make the journey from the
surrounding villages and countryside, in which, as in many
counties, a large number of the village schools are Church
foundations. Once these children have been admitted, others
living in the locality of the school whose families do not belong
to the Church of England take the remaining places. The Diocese
is proud of its new school, the reputation of which is high; and
co-operation with the local education authority (which had to
agree to make a place in its overall provision for the new voluntary school) was and is harmonious. This situation means that
the school draws on a substantial proportion of intelligent and
well motivated families who are prepared to do a great deal to
help the school do its best for their children. In this way the
school perhaps has a flying start over some of the others considered in this chapter; it is also probably under keener scrutiny

from the interested parties. On transfer at 13, the pupils of St. Wulstan's join those from the two county middle schools at the Underdown upper school. There are high-ranking independent schools within reach, and a few pupils are moved to them by their parents at the age of 11, frequently to the regret of both the school and the pupils themselves.

Premises

St. Wulstan's replaced the upper years of two Church primary schools in the town and of two small nearby village schools, the diocesan authorities being anxious not to lose the distinctive influence which they believe good church schools give to their pupils as early as the age of 9; the county education authority willingly accepted that this contribution should continue. None of the four primary schools was capable of expansion and modernising to the required standards for a middle school; consequently St. Wulstan's has the benefit of a pleasant and spacious new site on the edge of the town, and of course of entirely new buildings. Happily, the architect commissioned was familiar with designing schools and was anxious to draw on the experience of the county education authority's architects as well as compile his specification in conjunction with a group of heads and teachers, some of whom had clear ideas about the new opportunities which they thought school buildings should provide. Cost limits, as always, exercised a restraining hand, but the buildings themselves and the use of the site incorporate many of the ideas generally designated 'progressive' today.

To start with the outside, the designers were not satisfied to provide simply games pitches and a tarmac area. These are there, though the tarmac is larger and the games pitches fewer than customary; the tarmac is marked out for netball, shinty and other small-scale games, and adjoining it are two hard tennis courts, on which for teaching purposes quite a large group of pupils can receive instruction together. The buildings are grouped almost in one corner of the site; towards the opposite corner was a small spinney on ground sloping slightly away, and, instead of felling, clearing, and levelling, the designers retained these features to provide a school nature reserve which has proved its value as a real study resource. The remaining ground is divided between pitches for the more space-hungry games (football, hockey, cricket) and unobstructed grass areas where gymnastics, dance, and outdoor drama can take place; a semi-circular screen of bushes and shrubs has already grown sufficiently to give the effect of a backcloth to a stage. Finally, there is sufficient green strip around the perimeter of the site to permit pupils to stroll right round during their lunch hour if they wish—with the exception of the nature reserve, which is entered only under supervision.

The use of the grounds is imaginative. That so much can be got on to them is partly due to the grouping of the buildings at one corner and to their compact design which has made economical use of ground space. The traditionalist might object that the team games have suffered from this lay-out; the new vintage of physical education specialist would reply that breadth of experience is as important in the upper years of the middle school age range as is team experience, and that in the crowded land that Britain now is participation in games which need less space and fewer players is to be encouraged. At St. Wulstan's this approach can, over the next few years, certainly be fairly tested.

The buildings themselves are grouped around a central courtyard, made pleasant by flower beds, shrubs and plants grown in tubs, and a goldfish pool; all of these adjuncts are used as teaching aids by the environmental studies department. Around the courtyard, and separated from it by glass screens with doors, run, first, an inner belt and then an outer belt of rooms and spaces. There is very little space given to corridors or sheer circulation space; adults and pupils are expected to be able to move quietly through working spaces without disturbing those in them, and on this assumption the greater part of the building has become working space. Access is not, however, unrestricted to laboratories and workshops, where safety factors are paramount; these are so located that there is no need for through traffic and that those entering them do so through a proper door-way. Similarly, staff and administrative rooms are enclosed in the traditional way.

The inner belt around the courtyard consists of dining space on two sides, the library (not enclosed but in part divided up into working bays) on the third, and display and bench areas in connection with the decorative domestic arts and crafts on the fourth. This belt is approximately 14 feet wide. Around it are on the first side the administrative rooms and main entrance with foyer; on the second is a block considerably longer than the inner belt and housing the kitchen (with direct access to the dining areas), the main hall, an adjoining small hall, and changing rooms and stores; on the third (the library side) there is as yet no building, but instead access through two doors to a sheltered outdoor paved area which lies between the small hall on the one side and a classroom block on the other; and on the fourth is a large workshop area equipped for woodwork at one end, for environmental science at the other, and for clay and similar modelling crafts between. A noise screen is provided between the woodwork and the clay modelling areas by stores and the small room housing the pottery kiln.

Projected from the corners where this workshop area meets the first and the third sides are two square classroom blocks, each of two floors; access to them is by short enclosed corridors with stairs to the upper floor. Each floor serves a complete year group as base; it consists of three classrooms, one of which is fully walled and can be shut off therefore for either noisy activities or those requiring complete quiet. The other two are open to a central working area, though sliding partitions can close them off when this is necessary.

On the upper floor, over the workshop area already described, is a generous enclosed area of the same size which is equipped for science and mathematics. The picture is completed at present by a ground floor extension from the environmental science laboratory itself which is of lighter construction and provides a heated greenhouse and an animal husbandry room. The next section, on organisation, gives some idea of how the school work is actually distributed among the various rooms and blocks.

Organisation and Curriculum

It is the firm belief of the head, in which most of his staff follow him, that the middle school should establish its own identity as an educational institution and that schools which, like his own, are blessed with good premises and facilities ought to be the pioneers and pacemakers. It is the aim of the school to offer something more than did its predecessors, the junior schools and the lower forms of secondary schools. This is to be attained through three main approaches. The first is that child development and curricular development should proceed as a smooth evolving process throughout the years from 9 to 13, and that all teachers should see this as a continuous evolution; so far as possible, therefore, every teacher should do some work in both the early and the later years. The second is that teaching and learning in the school should be based on an integrated curriculum, and that team teaching is a necessary technique if this is to be achieved. The third is that, especially in a district where parental interest is so keen, definite efforts should be made both to inform parents of what the school is doing and why, and, further, to give them opportunities to join in its life both outside the classroom and at times inside.

The first approach has led to an interlocking organisation whereby most teachers belong to both a year group and a subject team. Each of the first three years is organised in three classes with a team of four teachers, one of whom acts as tutor group leader ('tutor group' is the title employed by the school instead of the more usual 'class'). Since each tutor also has a subject teaching assignment with another year, it does not often happen that all four tutors are there together—though a subject teacher from another year may be there in exchange for the temporarily absent member. The term 'head of department' is not used, but in each subject team one teacher is designated to be responsible for equipment, supplies, the special room where there is one, and for convening subject meetings as required; but, so far as new development within the subject is concerned, the hope is that all members will contribute, and in the head's view it is often those most recently out of college who should be best able to talk about current trends and findings. In the fourth year the general organisational principles are the same, though time-tabling gives a specific ten periods a week to be divided between mathematics and French, in which subjects the pupils are setted (ie re-grouped according to their degree of talent and attainment). Additionally, there are four tutor groups instead of three; the object of this is to reduce the size of the group which each tutor is expected to know intimately, so that a detailed profile of the pupils can be built up to ensure that the best advice is given to the upper school about each individual pupil when they transfer there at the end of the fourth year. This profile is concerned with personality, attainment, strengths, problems and potential; it begins with the group tutor who is responsible for keeping full contact with all the teachers who come to his group during the year, and is added to, or refined, by the tutor group leader and the headmaster.

The second approach, that of basing teaching and learning on an integrated curriculum and team teaching, in some ways looks to the primary developments embodied in the Plowden Report; but there is in fact a substantial amount of specialist teaching in several subjects requiring expert teachers (it may be said that the school is fortunate to have recruited them, but it offered clear job descriptions which proved attractive.) French, mathematics, environmental science, physical education and music all have specialist teachers who spend the greater part of their time teaching these subjects, much of it—though not all—to the third and fourth years in which they also belong to one of the tutor group teams. The search for an integrated curriculum therefore has usually to be initiated by the tutor group leaders, whose task it then is to enthuse their colleagues with the possibilities of a particular topic or study and to meet with them to co-ordinate what they are doing—not just once, but at least weekly throughout the particular study. In practice, to teachers who do not feel tied to a particular syllabus and to developing their subject in a particular way at a particular time, this is not as difficult as it sounds. To take a single example, a third year study of Greek civilisation which figured in no syllabus at all until a television documentary fired a member of the team who was an amateur archaeologist in his spare time, finally brought together the originator (actually the woodwork master) with his romantic narratives of Mycenae and Knossos, the English teacher with Homer in E. V. Rieu's translations and with resultant free writing by the pupils, the visiting drama teacher who set about a play on the wooden horse of Troy, which in turn soon brought in the music, dance and visual arts staff—while a side-track which arose from calculations on the number of men and ships engaged in the Trojan War led to a study by one group of mathematics in the ancient world. On one aspect and another, the study of the legends and civilisation of Greece continued through the greater part of a term and ended with public performances of the play which had brought so many sides of learning together and in which every pupil in the year took part.

It goes without saying that such an approach could easily lead to pupils assimilating a patchwork of knowledge in which, though subjects might have been integrated with each other in such topics as the one quoted, within each subject the range of their knowledge might be scrappy and uncoordinated. Theoretically, for instance, a pupil might have learned a great deal about Greek history and nothing whatever about the history of his own land; while the knowledge so acquired of one great civilisation would be of value, most parents and teachers would nevertheless regard his historical education as incomplete if by the age of 13 it included nothing of his native islands. Moreover, in the Greek study much of the work was done in groups engaged on different tasks, and all pupils did not therefore emerge with the same knowledge. This danger is less acute in some subjects, particularly mathematics, French and woodwork, where certain sequences are necessary to progress. But the conclusion is that careful records need not only be kept but scrutinised at the end of each term, so that the tutor group leaders and subject advisers consider together whether the ground of learning covered by particular groups and pupils is or is not getting badly out of balance. In some subjects the staff have drawn up basic lists of skills and of areas of knowledge which it is desirable to ensure are covered during a particular year and which act as a kind of check-list for the use of teachers and especially of the group tutors who are responsible for taking the overall view. Even here, the key word is 'desirable', not 'essential'; the staff generally agree both that pupils' capacities and modes of learning differ enormously and that one ought not to prescribe too rigidly, and also that in many subjects there is no set order in which bodies of facts have to be learned—though the attitudes and methods of working of pupils do need to be judged and to change as they mature.

The third approach consists of both informing parents what the school is doing and why, and engaging their active co-operation so far as possible. This is still experimental ground for most schools, and St. Wulstan's is no exception. A combination of means is found most effective. The school attaches much importance to its Parent-Teacher Association, and the ideas of parents are actively sought on the committee and indeed at any time about fresh areas of action. The regular meetings alternate between social and more strictly educational programmes, and the latter are by no means confined to lectures and talk. When many parents confessed their mystification at modern mathematics, for instance, two evening sessions were arranged in the mathematics rooms in which staff demonstrated the use of new apparatus and methods and parents then used them—proceeding from initial bafflement to an increasing understanding of what their children were actually doing in school. Similar or appropriately modified sessions have been held in science, environmental studies, and domestic subjects; on other occasions explanations have been given about such cardinal matters (to this school) as integration in the curriculum and team teaching.

The reverse side of the medal is what parents can do for the school. Here admittedly the school is fortunate in the large number of professions and leisure interests represented among its parents, but the head and his staff have lost no opportunity of turning such expertise to advantage. Mountaineering has been demonstrated by a leading climber complete with equipment; air/sea rescue by a former member of the service who was able to bring along a former comrade-in-arms still serving; the art of collage was demonstrated more than once by a mother who is one of its leading exponents at national level; a visit to Whipsnade Zoo has been led by a Fellow of the Zoological Society. The head believes he has a long way to go yet before he exhausts the resources of his parent power, and there is no doubt of the enthusiasm so generated among the pupils.

Time-tabling may be an incidental, but great care is taken with it, for it is one of the means of holding a sound balance between the different branches of learning. The developmental subjects—those which require regular practice and something of a sequence in their teaching—are time-tabled in each year in which they are taught with a definite number of periods per week. French, music, woodwork, physical education, and domestic subjects, which all have a definite range of skills to be mastered, come under this heading; and mathematics is added in the fourth year. When their needs for time have been met, the remaining aspects of the child's learning are in the hands of the tutor group leaders, who in the main simply time-table large blocks of time for their teams to cover English, history, geography, science, environmental studies, art and craft, and religious education. Much of the actual work is done on a team basis, some of it is integrated in topics, some is taught separately. There is good scope for a combination of the pastoral rôle exercised by the group tutor towards his group and of initiative by individual teachers involving either simply their own work or that of others in co-operation with them. The second feature governing time-tabling is of course that the specialist rooms for science, woodwork, domestic subjects and environmental studies have to be allocated to specific groups at fixed periods, as do the two halls in which music, drama, and indoor physical education take place.

Staff

St. Wulstan's is generously staffed, partly because it is the policy of the county education authority to encourage experiment in its new schools and partly because the year groups were originally expected to be larger than in fact they are. A staff of 19 full-time teachers in addition to the head, plus six part-timers who in all equate to a little over 3 full-timers, gives a present ratio of one teacher to 19 pupils. The attractions of a new and well designed and equipped school under a head who was prepared to experiment have drawn staff of high quality, many with considerable experience. They are inclined to think, talk and act together to such good purpose that it is now difficult to tell which came from primary and which from secondary work— a sure sign that they are achieving the head's object of producing a coherent and progressive educational programme throughout the middle years. At the same time the curricular cover is extremely good; there is no subject taught in the school which does not have a teacher with specialist knowledge, either by formal qualification or acquired by long experience. Music and remedial education are greatly helped by part-timers.

In a sense, the head can hardly believe his luck; yet a cloud is on the horizon. This is the question of incentives—not so much within the school, where it is possible to make a reasonable distribution of 'scale posts' to reward the most responsible positions, as in prospects of further promotion outside. The most original and active teachers are mainly in their thirties or early forties and naturally are seeking promotion, or will shortly do so. The head's concern is with the lack of promotion posts in middle schools generally for such teachers, who in practical terms are probably limited to applying for headships and deputy headships, of which there are all too few. The risk incurred in appointing a young and active staff is that, if they do not succeed in moving up the ladder, they may become spent volcanoes in the one school. Against this has to be set the risk that, if they do succeed in moving, their precise specialisms or combination of qualities may prove difficult to replace. The latter is the lesser risk, since at least it ensures that the school does not become frozen in its organisation but has to face change.

Conversation with the staff reveals two gaps, as they feel them to be, in supporting provision. The first is shortage of funds for outside visits by parties of pupils, varying from the local half-day visit to a neighbouring pre-historic earthwork or stately home to a full week spent studying the geology, ecology and landscape of the Lake District. This feeling speaks volumes for the enthusiasm of the staff and for the breadth of their view of what constitutes education; but there is little likelihood of any easement. The second is of adequate in-service training relevant to middle school teachers, most teachers' courses being in their view designed for either primary or secondary teachers and evading the issues between. This feeling partakes almost of a 'divine discontent' in that there is certainly no imminent or easy solution; indeed, middle school teachers elsewhere, in areas where this kind of pioneering approach has not taken place, might wish to turn to colleagues like those at St. Wulstan's to learn what is being found feasible. Certainly planned approaches are following with zest, new curricular directions are explored, and the school looks, listens and learns.

Achievement

This is both easy and difficult to sum up. By any commonly accepted standard, the work produced by the pupils in this school is rarely less than satisfactory and at its best is original, well produced and inspiring. Few weaknesses will be found among either the average or the bright children in the basic skills of language, mathematics and computation. They are in general articulate, competent and at times sparkling on paper, accustomed to problem solving and interested in new challenges. They are capable of sustained attention to one topic for a long time, are capable of working effectively on their own, are often voracious readers and/or markedly interested in the practical and physical skills. The school's music, drama, and work with the natural environment is probably outstanding. Nor do the less able children seem, in general, either forgotten or ill at ease; much of their teaching takes place in small groups in quiet places and it is liberally interspersed with enjoyable activities such as games, drama and art work for which they form part of larger groups.

What is less easy to define is how typical this school can ever be. It is well endowed as regards location, premises, equipment and staff; it is well led by a head who wrote the blueprint for, and continues to appraise and inspire, all that goes on; and it is supported by a largely appreciative and intelligent body of parents and friends. It can be fairly said that it is a true pace-maker and that its achievement matches its opportunities; what has still to be learned is how such achievement can be transferred to the main stream of education.

School F *Name:*   Fairbridge First and Middle School
         Location: Fairbridge, County of Easthamshire
         Age range: 5 to 12
         Roll: 180, of whom 105 are in the 8 to 12
                          classes.
         History: Until four years ago a 5 to 11 primary
                          school, when in accordance with the
                          county reorganisation plan the age
                          range was extended to 12 and the
                          school re-named.

Area served

Fairbridge is a large village in a prosperous agricultural county,
clustered around a medieval church and manor house. At the

turn of the century it must have been largely self-contained and self-sufficient, with the majority of workers employed in farming or on the manor estate. To-day fewer than half can find occupation in or around the village, but the county town eight miles away compensates for the lack of any industry in the village itself; its inhabitants look there not only for employment but for much of their shopping and services. The school serves also three or four hamlets and a considerable number of outlying farms. In the last dozen years a fair amount of new housing has been erected, mainly in small clusters. The social mix has always been easy, and the scatter of professional families accounts for a good deal of local leadership, including interest in education and particularly in the school.

This school exemplifies many of the features and problems of the combined school (as such joint First and Middle schools are usually known). It is much the smallest of the schools studied in this chapter, and indeed the number of pupils of the middle school age range in it only slightly exceeds 100. Circumstances meant that the incentive to establish a clear middle school identity was far less forceful than in the others; the education authority followed two guiding principles in its reorganisation plans, first to keep the size of its secondary schools reasonably small (retaining the 11 to 12 age group in middle or combined schools obviously helped) and second to put into practice as much as was practicable of the Plowden Report's recommendations on primary education—of which the later age of 12 as the transfer point to secondary education was one. Part of the price paid to achieve this, in the rural parts of the county as distinct from the towns, was the need to adopt combined schools as the only practical method; the building of new 'area' middle schools serving an extensive area and depending on a costly school transport network was considered, but it was evident that the necessary central funds for such a major programme would not be granted. Moreover, though the residents of the rural areas had some apprehensions about the change, they had even more about their village schools being reduced to first schools only.

Premises

Fairbridge Primary School had grown over the best part of a century. The original building consisted, as did many of its period, of three classrooms separated by folding partitions and which could therefore be thrown into one for either school or village occasions, and one adjoining but self-contained room for the infants. Later additions included two modern classrooms, a small but useful and attractive hall, and a kitchen, while the last of the numerous post-war bulges was contained by a pre-fabricated classroom in the playground. Finally, when the school was converted to its present status, the education authority installed a *conversion unit*. also in the playground, con-sisting of one large room (approximately 1,000 sq. ft.) equipped with water, sinks, calor gas and electricity, and a capacious store-room. The total effect is of a heterogeneous collection of build-ings, giving plenty of space for the 180 children now on roll (in-deed, up to a further sixty would be admitted without any question of further accommodation) but lacking any unity of design. The older parts of the buildings are short of storage space, and, though a series of minor works has provided a reasonable staff room and a room which has to serve both the head and his secretary, the arrival of parents or other visitors desiring a private interview presents difficulties. The older rooms have been attractively re-decorated and well equipped with dis-play boarding and lightweight modern furniture; and the folding partition between two of the original classrooms is now left more or less permanently open in the presence of two teachers who, with consecutive age groups, like to work together.

The playground is congested by the additional buildings and the games which can be played upon it are consequently limited. The school has the use of an adjoining public recreation field and does not appear to find the restrictions irksome. Team games such as football and cricket suffer more from the small number of older boys (netball is less seriously affected) than from the restrictions of space. The nearest swimming facilities are in the county town, and school visits are so time-consuming, even when the pools can make room, that they are rarely undertaken. On the other hand, opportunities for natural history and for a variety of local studies are right on the doorstep, so that the school's location has advantages as well as handicaps.

Organisation

The head is of course responsible for the whole of the combined school, not merely for the 'middle school' part of it; and indeed neither in attitude nor in formal organisation is the barrier between the two component parts any more marked than in the old days of infants and juniors. This makes for a friendly family feeling; but it also reduces the opportunities directly available to the pupils of middle school age—at least, in comparison with some of the other schools we have studied. The three infant classes have the use of the original building, roughly speaking; this leaves the four middle years classes with the two other older classrooms, the pre-fabricated room, the conversion unit, and part use of the hall. A medical inspection room, when not in use for this purpose, is used for small group work. The entrance lobby to the pre-fabricated room, originally intended as a cloak-room, has been taken over as a small but useful library.

A generation ago one would have regarded these facilities for a junior school with some satisfaction; but for middle schools in the 1970s, judgement has to be different. They are designed for a basic class teaching organisation, with little movement by each class out of its own room. Problems of display and of storage implicit in to-day's teaching methods are not easily solved. The hall gives space for physical education, with light portable ap-paratus but without fixed gymnasium equipment, for music and for drama, and each class can count on using the hall at least once during the day. The conversion unit affords facilities for work in science (using a minimum of apparatus), for art and some crafts, for practical mathematics, and for some project work requiring more table-top space than the classrooms can provide; and all of this is useful provision. The head quite rightly allows priority of access to this unit to the oldest group, which a few years ago would no longer have been here but would have been enjoying the superior facilities of secondary schools in the county town.

His main problem is how to give enough variety and curricular challenge to this group, and especially to the ablest children in it. Indeed, in the last two years of the course it is unlikely that any one teacher will be able to satisfy all their needs, and in the other schools we have studied the heads have been careful, in recruiting staff, to build up expert knowledge in all main aspects of the curriculum. The difficulty in the small combined school is obvious. The school has eight classes, four in the first school and four in the middle school range. Though none are large and the teachers' task is thereby easier than in many schools, nevertheless the four who work with the youngest classes can be called on but little to help with the older—even if they command the right kind of expertise. The school is not ungenerously staffed by any means (a strictly statistical calculation in fact shows a ratio of one teacher to nineteen pupils), but the teaching resources available to the four older classes are their four class teachers, two half-timers who specialise in drama and remedial education, and a visiting member of the county's team of peripatetic music teachers. At one time French was offered, also taken by a peripatetic teacher; this was a brave attempt by the authority to provide a foreign language in what were then its junior schools, but when the teacher moved to another post the recruitment of a successor proved impossible, and the curriculum does not now include French. Fortunately the four class teachers among them cover English, religious education, art and craft, science, and environmental studies with some measure of skill, while the head himself is a keenly interested historian. So far the pupils fare reasonably well; but the gaps, apart from French, are in practical studies (woodwork and cookery, for instance), in the restricted nature of the art and craft, and in mathematics where, though basic work is covered without difficulty, more advanced features which would be within the reach of the ablest children cannot be included.

Achievement

This was until four years ago a conventional primary school; in many respects it still is. No-one who has seen good primary schools will be unduly worried about that; but from the curricular gaps just noted it is evident that children from Fairbridge cannot fail to be handicapped, on entering their next school, in comparison with those from larger town middle schools. The greatest difficulty that has emerged in the four years is that of giving the oldest pupils sufficient challenge and staving off boredom, from which some certainly suffer. The avid readers (there are some) find too little in the library to keep them going; those in whom artistic gifts are emerging have too little chance to take up new skills and to receive the stimulus of well-informed help with them. In music the story is different; several of the staff are musical and interest, in the lunch hour as well as in lesson time, runs high, and the visiting music specialist also gives instrumental tuition to quite large groups from each of the four middle school years. Science, based in the main on enquiry methods, the use of simple apparatus, and careful observation of natural phenomena in the countryside, both interests and informs the majority of pupils, but there are certainly some in the older groups who could benefit by training in laboratory techniques and by more rigorous presentation of some aspects of scientific study. Mathematics again suffers from having no well qualified academic mathematician to stretch the mental capacities of the really bright twelve-year old. Some of the parents in the professional classes express anxiety over these aspects of the local reorganisation, contrasting them unfavourably with the earlier situation in which able twelve-year olds were attending the town grammar schools; and, even though this view overlooks the fact that the secondary schools too have been reorganised and are not what they were, the parents point to the fact that both qualified staff and specialist accommodation are nevertheless to be found in them.

The majority of parents remain satisfied with what the school does; some even prefer having their children within the village setting for an additional year, particularly since the former secondary schools have expanded in size and may be more daunting than before to a country-bred twelve year old. Basically, the school remains an extended primary school with slightly better facilities and staffing than it enjoyed in its former role, but certainly without much of the range and challenge which well-designed purpose-built middle schools can offer. And, in a time of economic stringency, both the head and the more perceptive of his parents wonder anxiously how long it will be before the existing staffing ratios are worsened, and what effect any reduction will have on the school's ability to cover its curriculum.

CHAPTER 7

The Present Situation: an analysis

The six schools described in the foregoing chapter (not actual schools, it will be recalled, but amalgams of typical schools) are sufficiently representative to illustrate the present over-all situation. The pace-maker schools, with their great promise and their already considerable achievements, are there; and, if they are not yet numerous, there are enough of them to show what middle schools can be. At the other end of the scale are more schools than one would like to admit which are hampered by poor facilities, inadequate preparation for their new rôle, and staffs who fail to understand the potential of the well led and well motivated middle school. In between is the whole width of the educational spectrum.

The range of the spectrum

There are certainly a number of schools like Aurora, which, aided by well designed premises which lend themselves to a variety of teaching approaches, have confidently built upon the philosophy and practices expounded in the Plowden Report. There are others which, like Millrace, base their objectives not on primary but on liberal secondary traditions and practices. There are yet others like Meadowvale which aim at combining the best of both primary and secondary traditions; and, more rarely, there are others like St. Wulstan's which set out simply to mould a school appropriate to the age range and the backgrounds of the children who come to them and to use to the full the facilities provided and the talents of the staffs. So far, we have neither uniformity nor any clear sign that any of these approaches is unsuitable.

Facilities

Some have been designed with particular educational aims and approaches in view, and on the basis of wide consultation; others, like Victoria and Fairbridge, are housed in old buildings erected to the specifications of a bygone generation long past when educational and social thought was very different from that of to-day. The new site and buildings at St. Wulstan's seem to offer a school almost everything it could need; Fairbridge, in contrast, has to make do with a patchwork of additions to a Victorian village school. The conversion of Meadowvale from a traditional secondary modern building to its present form as a 9 to 13 middle school has been imaginatively executed with major alterations and additions; whereas at Victoria, with its uncertain length of life and grim industrial surroundings, all that has been undertaken is the minimum necessary to keep it in service for a slightly different age-range and an uncertain period of time. Many middle schools can look and plan ahead; those like Victoria cannot.

The educational possibilities in purpose-built schools like Millrace and St. Wulstan's are in fact a world away from those in schools like Victoria or Fairbridge. In the first two, specialist rooms or bases are available for science, wood and metalwork, art and craft, and domestic subjects such as cookery and needlecraft; there is easy access to audio-visual aids such as film and strip projectors, television sets, record players and the like, either in a special room or in rooms easily adapted for their use; there is a well housed library, in some cases serviced by a full or part-time library assistant; there are outdoor facilities for rural science, weather recording, and natural history, and in one for outdoor drama and dance. Virtually none of these are to be found in Victoria or Fairbridge. Moreover, the lively teaching techniques and methods which are often stimulated by good facilities are equally out of reach; team teaching, co-operation between departments on large-scale projects, individual assignments involving free movement by pupils around the school, and the excitement of dramatic and musical productions by large groups, are just not possible.

Staffing

The balance of staffing resources is similarly weighted—not necessarily in the sheer mathematical figure of pupil/teacher ratio itself where, for instance, Fairbridge showed one of the most favourable of all—but in reckoning the actual total resources which the teaching power of the staff gives, and, even more important, their quality. We have seen in Fairbridge how handicapped the small combined school, in particular, can be, with effective total resources for its middle school classes of only six full-time teachers and perhaps a little help for a small proportion of the week from others. This figure is quite below what is needed to cover in an informed way the full curriculum of English, mathematics, religious education, social studies (or history and geography separately), science and environmental studies, physical education, a wide variety of art and crafts, domestic subjects, wood and metalwork and possibly French and rural science. The good primary teacher may be willing to try anything (indeed, our educational system owes a great deal to such teachers) but they clearly cannot match the actual knowledge and expertise available to schools like Meadowvale and Millrace, with their 28 full-time or equivalent teachers. With an establishment of this size, a school can set out to attract really well qualified specialist, as well as general, teachers. Victoria and Fairbridge have no such chance.

It is difficult to define what produces a staff of high calibre; but the cheerful excitement, buoyancy, confidence and open-mindedness of a school which has one is easily recognised. There are a great many hardworking, talented and dedicated teachers holding the educational (and social) line in schools like Victoria; but the enterprising teacher, anxious to try out new curricular initiatives and to enjoy the co-operation of like-minded colleagues, naturally turns elsewhere. And the ultimate attainments of the pupils are bound to reflect superior working conditions and quality of staff. Schools cannot, realistically, all be equal; but how big are the gaps?

Equality of Opportunity: the dilemma

It would be quite unfair to expect all middle schools to be beacons of progress. What is remarkable is that so many are—and the pacemakers can set the pace for the next generation. Meanwhile, it does no service to deny the existence of some which are dull, restricted in outlook, and doing little to keep abreast of research or to take advantage of new curricular material. There are many teachers on middle school staffs who had no wish to be there and would have preferred to remain in the familiar junior or secondary school; they have been caught up in a reorganisation for which they were not responsible and which they view without enthusiasm. They will continue to do, for the most part, a sound job along the lines they have known, but one looks to them in vain for new initiatives. And, in the nature of things, this may be as true of the leadership as of the assistant staff. Not all heads are convinced that the middle school offers anything new which is of value; some prefer to stick to the aims and the methods of working they know and trust; some have no great interest in curriculum development or consider it unrelated to the needs of their own school; some feel they get little practical support from above. They have a point of view with which one can sympathise; but the dilemma remains. In a land which for a generation and more has honestly pursued the ideal of equal educational opportunity for all, it is sad to have to record that even in the new world of the middle school this manifestly does not exist. Our hope lies in the pacemaker schools, which show what can be done; the problem is how to do it.

So is equality of opportunity then a will o' the wisp? Some would say it is; that too many factors militate against it; that the opportunities open to children depend on where they live, and that this in turn depends on the socio-economic class into which they were born, the ambition of their parents for them, the priorities of local councils in taking hard decisions of policy and finance, and the heritage of the area in terms of both outlook and buildings. We have seen how the introduction of the middle school reflected two main motives—one, that of a desire for educational progress in the light of new knowledge, the other, the stimulus of political expediency, making use of middle schools in order to advance secondary re-organisation on the comprehensive principle rather than making them possible for any virtues of their own.

There is however no call to take a cynical view of such decisions. In the nature of things, the majority of educational buildings in the country are always old and, to a varying extent, outliving their usefulness; nevertheless they have to continue in use until the country can afford to replace them. In some areas such as new towns or large new residential estates new schools have to be erected anyway and the opportunity, given wise planning and good design, then arises to give the fortunate children of the area in question the kind of educational experience open to them at Aurora, Millrace, or St. Wulstan's. In others—the inner belt areas of many cities, for instance, where the shape of ultimate reconstruction is not clear or where it depends on some distant financial future—the most well intentioned of authorities operates under severe constraints. To rebuild Victoria, in an area which may eventually cease to be residential at all, is a gamble no authority could take even were the Department of Education and Science approval for such a course likely—which, in the continuing competition for scarce resources, it certainly would not be. Perhaps the fairest judgement is that schools are victims of the speed of change. The question is whether they are going to become forgotten victims. Faced with schools like these, it is no wonder if in a great many middle school areas both educationists and parents are asking what, after all, is so new and promising about middle schools. It is therefore of great importance both to evaluate the work being done in the best of the middle schools, to judge how far their approaches are transferable to the less well provided schools, and to establish the basic minima of staffing, resources, objectives and support without which it is unreasonable and unfair to set up middle schools at all. Such an evaluation is made in the next chapter.

CHAPTER 8

What have Middle Schools achieved?
An evaluation

Aims

We have taken a bird's eye view of sample schools in action. What do the schools themselves consider their aim and purpose? If these are not both clear and capable of attainment, achievement will be haphazard. Some of the best LEAs acknowledged this to the extent of appointing the heads of their prospective earliest middle schools a year or more before they opened, and in many cases in relieving them of other duties for part or all of this period. These fortunate heads were thus able to devote their energies fully to identifying aims, planning means, and working out detail in conjunction with the teachers, especially the senior ones, who were to join their staffs. In areas where total or large-scale reorganisation was to take place on the same date, these preparatory single school exercises were supplemented by wider discussions, by short courses, conferences, and working parties, usually arranged or supported by the authority's advisory and in-service training services and often by other agencies as well.

From the experience and records (though paper records have often been discarded once their job is done) of schools and areas which prepared in this way it is evident that two convictions were widely held. The first, to draw on a figure of speech already quoted, was that middle schools must develop their own identity and not regard themselves as either an elongated junior school or a kind of educational pantomime horse with one pair of primary and one pair of secondary legs and no clear idea about where the whole animal is to go. The second was complementary; that aims and objectives must be based on knowledge of how children develop and learn, and that the practical means of attaining these aims must be worked out in detail, assessed continuously, and modified as experience dictated. These means were the curricular and pastoral structures, the criteria for judging pupil performance, and the records, liaison, and administrative procedures. Schools which have carried these intentions into action usually run smoothly and can see themselves critically.

These groups produced a great deal on paper, especially when primary and secondary teachers met jointly to study, for example, the development of a particular subject of the curriculum, ways of integrating several subjects, or the deployment of staff best suited to what they had in mind. From this kind of working party grew organisational features such as year teams and consultant teachers, together with a firm acknowledgement of the interdependence not only of different fields of knowledge but also of middle and upper schools, if the educational process was to be smooth and continuous.

Few of these documents were circulated other than locally, for it was local situations with which they dealt; but much of the thinking was more widely applicable. Fortunately views did get exchanged at national courses and conferences and common features of a middle school approach were consequently built up. In the schools themselves the early documents, valuable when produced, were superseded within two or three years by others drawing upon the practical experience of running the schools. This is in fact a measure of their success, for the function of such studies is to crystallize thought and discussion. It is surely no accident that the heads of the first generation of the pacemaker schools were men and women who gave the best kind of leadership, that of taking the staff into their confidence, promoting discussion, and securing a substantial measure of agreement on policies, practices and procedures. These heads displayed great skill in rendering the school's aims and guidelines into language which all could understand and interpret in their own areas of work. Undoubtedly they had their own vision of what the middle school could become; and our education service is deeply in their debt for what their schools have accomplished.

Cold quotation can only give imperfectly the flavour of such an essentially personal institution as a school; but some typical extracts from guideline papers will give an idea of the aims which successful middle schools have set themselves.

'The nine year old is a child and the thirteen year old is an adolescent. It is the job of the middle school to cater for this transition by moving gradually from the relatively unstructured situation through to a much more structured, though nevertheless flexible, approach. as the child's development dictates.'

'Our greatest challenge is one of establishing a truly meaningful education which will be sounder and more stimulating for the nine to thirteen year olds than the previous pattern. Obviously to begin with we must draw heavily on knowledge gained in the present organisation, but to be really successful we must produce a character and method of work which is uniquely our own and which is undoubtedly better for the children in terms of positive educational advantages.'

'As middle schools are new and are catering for a new age range, they naturally are forced into the forefront of curriculum development . . . . In Maths and Science, Communications, Modern Languages, Music, Art and Craft, and Physical Education the school must be seen by parents to be offering extra . . . .'

'The middle years are the years in which children not only discover themselves as people but develop attitudes towards studies in general and certain subject disciplines in particular. Their experience must include a growing mastery of working techniques but also a feeling for the relatedness of different areas of knowledge—and we have to teach them both self-confidence and self-criticism.'

'The school's policy is one of individual learning. Each child should encounter the full quota of individual subjects in any one week, but not necessarily at the same time or at the same level as his classmates. Stimuli can often be provided on a group basis; it is in developing from them that individual interests and talents have scope. Both the various resource centres in the school and what the children themselves offer are to be drawn upon . . . .'

---

and one extract which is not from a school document but from a design brief compiled by a working party of architects, administrators and teachers; the paragraph is entitled 'The Entity of the Middle School'.

The successful middle school will ensure that all levels of ability in each child can be given full scope for further growth and development. It should be a community with its own character, its own uniqueness and atmosphere and, despite the age range it embraces, it must evolve as an entity in itself without trace of any dichotomy of primary and secondary. It should be centred around the child as an individual and should allow him to mature at his own pace, to foster his individual type of learning, to give him the opportunity to discover and foster his own interests, to be capable of working harmoniously with others in groups, to learn how to learn and to acquire the necessary skills to enable him to make progress commensurate with his ability.

These quotations very fairly represent the starting point of the best middle schools. How far have they been achieved, and what kind of performance have they led to?

Criteria of Assessment; internal and external

How is performance to be assessed, especially in the case of schools which put stress on individual achievement rather than on class or group norms? Six main means are available, none of them entirely satisfactory.

(i) *Externally directed examinations* These offer a ready-made yardstick at the ages of, say, 15 to 18, when the General Certificate of Education (Ordinary and Advanced levels) and the Certificate of Secondary Education play an important, though not an un-challenged, part. But there are none in the middle school years—nor do staffs show any enthusiasm for them.

(ii) *Standardised tests* Most middle schools make some use of these to keep a check on such things as a child's reading ability and mathematical performance. They are useful in this context; but they can test only a narrow and specific area of competence, and large parts of the curriculum and of other school activity cannot be tested in this way. (The so-called *intelligence tests* need the most careful interpretation of all, and are rarely a guide to over-all performance.)

(iii) *Judgement of Upper School Staffs* The judgement of the staffs of the schools to which middle school children go on is certainly of value; but it is limited, depending on what these staffs expect (and this is likely to be determined in the light of their own aims) and on the extent of their knowledge of what the aims of the middle schools are.

(iv) *Parental Judgement* This again is of considerable value and importance; it is rarely comparative in the sense that few parents will know how other schools are performing; and it too is influenced by their own expectations of their children and by the degree of their understanding of what middle schools are and what they are about.

(v) *Judgement of Middle School Staffs* The people doing the job certainly have a right to be heard. Probably most could fairly be described as pleased but not yet fully satisfied; and those who aim the highest are sometimes the severest critics of their own performance.

(vi) *Judgement of Professional Observers* In these days a large number of professional observers from other branches of education visit schools, especially new and interesting ones. (The visitors' books of some middle schools read like a gazetteer not only of the United Kingdom but of the world; Europe, North America, Australia, India, Singapore, Japan . . . . it sometimes seems as if the whole world is coming to look for successful middle schools!) Among them are local education authority inspectors and advisers, HM Inspectors, university and teacher training lecturers, and students training to teach. A substantial amount of professional judgement, though admittedly largely subjective and uncoordinated, is being built up, though to refine it into a consensus is difficult.

The assessments in the rest of this chapter are based to some extent on all six sources; it would also be surprising if there were not an element of personal subjective judgement.

Pupils as People: their Personal Development

Some years ago Stockwell College of Education in Bromley produced a film to be used in the training of student teachers entitled 'Children are People'. This battle-cry (for the title reflected the philosophy of an entire college staff) was a declaration that children are not some easily categorised species nor creatures to be parcelled and treated according to formulae for the convenience of adults, but that each one is an individual personality with actual and potential strengths, weaknesses, advantages and problems; that they differ in temperament and in home and social background, and that each one is entitled to the same care which responsible adults take in making their own relationships. The film went on to show how, in the classroom, individual children needed to be observed, talked to, encouraged, introduced progressively to new social situations, and taught both how and what to learn.

Judged by this standard—now widely accepted—the schools generally do well. The atmosphere, at work or play, is cheerful, friendly and confident. One strong feature of many well organised middle schools is the forming of different groups for different purposes, thus enlarging children's experience of their fellow human beings and helping them to learn techniques of co-operation. As they move up the school, an increasing amount of responsibility for planning and executing particular tasks is often left to the pupils, though equally it is a mark of the good school that these activities are in the teacher's eye and that, whether he looks at their progress for two minutes or half an hour (which on successive days may well happen) he knows what is afoot and is ready to intervene when help is needed. Older pupils are expected to present and comment on their work, or that of their group, to their fellows, whether the presentation draws on verbal, visual or other means. In the final year of the course these practices may become steadily more adult in scope and quality.

Such approaches encourage independence and initiative among pupils. This is good for them, but of course has its risks. The buoyant extrovert child can easily dominate a group, if not carefully held in check. The exceptionally able or talented child can be held back by the speed of the group and become bored or disruptive, unless steps are taken fully to engage his talents. The larger school, with teachers working in teams and with plentiful material resources, clearly has an advantage here, and year team and tutor group systems can work very much to the benefit of these children, who can draw on several sources of skill and knowledge. Similarly they can be evaluated by a team, not by a single teacher. The response and the mature, co-operative attitude of pupils generally, is one of the most striking successes of these approaches.

This is also evident in their enthusiastic but responsible

conduct outside the school on educational visits, and equally in their reception of visitors to the school. A party of local councillors, overseas educationists, or children from schools in another part of the country making an exchange visit—the pupils take them in their stride, acting as hosts, guides, interviewers. All these experiences, and many others, contribute to personal development and to the ability to live and work together as members of a community.

The biggest challenge in this direction was presented by the 11–12 and 12–13 year olds. Some teachers were apprehensive of their ability to cope with them, but in fact many have excelled. One useful opportunity many schools have given these older children is that of helping younger or backward children, at work, in play or sport, and on outside visits. This is often done without any formal structure, the pupils being encouraged to view it as part of normal living. Apart from advances such as these, the whole fashion of work in the upper years has led pupils towards longer periods of study concentrated on a particular task, has introduced them to the demands of specialist disciplines in many subjects, has stressed the need for well planned and careful presentation of work, and has encouraged them to set their own standards, the oversight of the teachers ensuring regular appraisal of their work. There is no doubt that in the best middle schools the transition from the early exploratory approaches to the later structured and more disciplined ones in the later years is accomplished with great benefit to the children. The resultant pride in achievement and easy personal relationship with those in authority are certainly signs of maturity. One meets confident, sensible, cheerful pupils, well equipped as people to go forward to the experiences which await them in the next stage of their education.

Individual Learning

Here, the record of the best middle schools is quite outstanding. In recent years, as was noted by the Plowden Report, the sheer quality and range of work in language and literature, in the arts, in physical education, dance and drama, and in science and environmental studies had surged forward in many junior schools. The question for middle schools was whether they would be able to maintain this impetus through the older age groups up to twelve or thirteen; the answer is that they have certainly done so. A visit to any middle school of this calibre presents the visitor from the moment of arrival with displays of work showing colour, craftsmanship and mastery of language; it introduces him to children able and often anxious to talk about the work on which they are engaged, especially if it is a project following a theme, though they will probably be equally willing to take him on a tour of the school and talk informatively about it as they go. He may enter a classroom in which the class, or a number of small groups, are conversing in French with a fluency which many of their predecessors had not achieved at a much later age in the former secondary school. He may be entertained to a performance of part singing, of wind instruments or brass band music items, of choral speaking or of free imaginative dance in which each child or group illustrates a given topic. He may visit the library, or a third or fourth year centre to be introduced to the records—written, photographic, taped—of last summer's visit by a school party to the Lake District or last spring's to Paris. And he will find that, though most of these were group or co-operative enterprises, the records made by each pupil are markedly individual—that they reflect experiences which have been enhanced because several people took part in them and set down their own impressions in different ways. The quality of some of this work has to be seen to be believed, and in terms of individuality, imagination, discernment and polish, it is well in advance of work which twelve and thirteen year old pupils were producing twenty years ago.

The Groundwork of Knowledge: the Basic Skills

Good schools of all types regard literacy and numeracy as

essential instruments in to-day's world; good middle schools are no exception. They rarely confine themselves to the instructional methods of the past, but their results are just as effective. It is unusual for any child, other than those with some form of learning handicap (and not all of them) to leave a middle school unable to read, to express himself intelligibly in speech and writing, and to apply the basic mathematics essential to daily living. Most pupils, of course, accomplish far more than this absolute minimum.

Basic literacy is certainly an aim; but the schools are not satisfied with this. Reading is not just a device; it is a means to an end, to opening the doors of knowledge. The skill is useless if it is not purposefully used. Most pupils can read when they enter middle schools; and for this majority the schools therefore concentrate on giving them the inducement and the means to use their skill more widely and effectively day by day. Hence arises the need for ample supplies of books and other reading matter, fiction and non-fiction, learned and light-hearted, books to study with the teacher and books to read alone. Moreover, this is a task in which to some degree all teachers join, for almost every subject has not only its own language but its own reading matter, whether enjoyable or purely instructional. It is as important, though in an entirely different way, to be able to read accurately instructions for a science experiment as to enjoy Kenneth Grahame or Charles Dickens.

Reading has to be progressive as the pupils mature. At the school they become able to tackle longer, more difficult and complicated books, to learn how to use some for reference only, to skip and to browse where appropriate, and indeed to cultivate those more advanced reading skills which in the past were often neglected once teachers were satisfied that a child's 'reading age' was not behind his chronological age. Only recently, partly under the influence of the Bullock Report *A Language for Life* has it been fully appreciated that a child's 'reading age' does no more than show that he is fitted to go on to the more advanced reading skills; it offers no assurance that he will do so unless the school plans it so. The pioneer middle schools, with their wealth of interests, their staffs eager to explore new areas of work and new topics of study, and their actual resources of books and other reading material, have not only produced children who can 'read', but have given a new depth of meaning to the word and achieved, in many cases, a new high water mark.

Reading is not an isolated language skill. Writing advances with it, but clearly the process has to be planned. If a child can read, he should also write; he has of course to master the actual manual skill, and this calls for both direct instruction and practice. Once this is done, he can write within the limits of the vocabulary and the grammar and sentence constructions which he has been reading. Indeed, he may go further, for he has the whole vocabulary of his spoken English, his daily conversation and experiences within the school, the home, his friendship groups, and his radio and television listening to draw upon. This range enlarges his writing, but often at the cost of some curiously unconventional spelling; for English, as many adults know only too well, is no neat phonetically written language. One of the more teasing problems which teachers face is whether to halt the flow in the interests of accuracy or to let it run in the interests of fluency. Most agree that there are times for both, but that in the earlier years fluency should generally precede accuracy; in the later middle school years systematic attempts to master the conventions of spelling do need to be made, and most middle schools are attempting to do this. The same is true of basic grammar. It is nevertheless their aim to ensure that fluency in these skills is matched by articulacy of speech.

Some children of course do enter the middle school unable to read. Handicaps vary from an inability to recognise the shapes of letters to an inability to build words and sentences in the mind quickly enough to read with confidence or enjoyment. The causes of poor reading performance are diverse; among them can be poor or unsystematic teaching, over-large classes, absences from school at critical periods, lack of parental interest, or the congenital mal-functioning of a controlling part of the brain. Some can be remedied, others not. The good middle school arranges various remedial measures. First comes liaison with the contributory First school to learn the pupil's history, supplemented by diagnostic reading tests. Second, the larger middle schools mostly have at least one teacher expert in the teaching of reading techniques, whose task usually includes advising colleagues as well as teaching the backward readers himself. Third, the actual organisation of internal remedial teaching may vary considerably. Some schools assign poor readers to a 'remedial' class, maybe serving one age group, maybe more; these classes are small so that the bulk of the work can be individual, and half or more of it is likely to be in the hands of the one teacher. Others leave poor readers in their normal classes for purposes which do not draw heavily upon these skills, but withdraw them for specific instruction and practice in reading for one or two sessions in the day. Others again, especially where open-plan designs of building permit three or four teachers to work together with perhaps a whole year group in sight, need no such formal arrangement since at intervals during the day a skilled teacher can easily take aside two or three children, or maybe a single one, for a few minutes of close tuition. Whichever method is adopted, it is supplemented with careful daily records, so that continuous diagnosis accompanies the teaching and a careful sequence of progress is maintained with each child.

The schools' concern for numeracy is probably equally great, though in the area of mathematics there is less general agreement about what should be learned, how and why. As with reading, middle schools can reasonably expect most entrants to have some mastery of basic computation and of simple mathematical concepts, but they need to plan special support for those who have not. They are concerned that in the 1970s mathematics shall not be thought of simply as computation but that it shall be seen as an area of concepts and ideas as well as of skills. Computation has to be mastered, certainly; but once it has been, there is no virtue in, for example, undertaking endless practice exercises in addition, subtraction, multiplication and division. The next logical stage is frequently to introduce their pupils to the various aids, such as desk or pocket calculators, which eliminate drudgery and save time for more advanced work.

Understanding concepts such as space, time, measurement, the relationships of numbers to each other, and the principles underlying commonly used formulae, is essential if pupils are to use mathematics with confidence and to see their way through the kind of multi-stage problems which face, for example, builders, structural designers, bankers, or astronomers. Much of the work reached in the fourth year of middle schools such as these is quite advanced and can be either theoretical or practical. It can also present intellectual challenges to which the mathematically gifted can rise, and is one valuable element in keeping the able children mentally stretched. To see a group work through the areas of mathematics involved, for instance, in designing, financing, and erecting a new town centre—the surveying, the siting, the planning of the public utilities' installations with calculation of the amounts of water, electric power and drainage involved, the quantity surveying, the manpower control, the flow charts, progress checks, diagrammatic and algebraic representations, is to realise how far able children can go and how the good middle school is capable of taking them. Where the schools are well staffed, mathematically speaking, these and similar results are found. The majority of the pupils may not get this far; but by the age of twelve or thirteen they have a working knowledge of arithmetical processes, the uses of simple algebra, certainly of geometry so far as the study of shapes, angles, dimensions, and the formulation of propositions is concerned, and will be able to make whatever calculations are necessary in their science and other subjects.

There remain, as in the case of reading, those children who enter the middle school with weak foundations or with no clear grasp of what they are learning tables or number bonds for. They need the same kind of careful day-to-day care as do the slow readers; frequently, in fact, they are the same pupils and will be taught by the same teacher. Remedial work in language and in mathematics does not, however, necessarily proceed at the same rate; some children do have more difficulty with one than with the other. There is a further problem found in many schools of pupils who are linguistically competent, sometimes very intelligent, and well ahead in much of their work but who, for whatever reason, are mathematically seriously behind. Their need is for a mathematics course which is really remedial, in which a skilled mathematician (who may or may not be a general remedial teacher) takes them effectively over the ground they may earlier have missed, or have covered without true understanding; the time that this takes varies with the degree of backwardness and with the motivation of the child. With some it can be concentrated and quick, for the intelligent child will often appreciate what is being done for him and why. Others, less well motivated or less confident, take much longer. In neither case, however, is the work limited to drill in tables and number bonds; it is accompanied by problems which demonstrate the importance of the drills. Such approaches are not yet universal, but are common enough to offer hope of overcoming the long-standing problem of weak performance in mathematics.

The Superstructure: what else do the pupils learn?

There is in this country no centrally controlled curriculum. Middle schools too are free from the constraints of externally directed examinations at the end of the course; they are, in a sense, responsible to no-one but themselves for the choice and range of the work they do. Further, the educational philosophy to which so many of them subscribe accepts, in the early years of their courses at least and often throughout, the need for pupils to explore, to experiment, to range widely into the field of human knowledge, to experience extensive rather than intensive learning. Class or group programmes are supplemented by a variety of individual assignments. Many teachers do not wish to subject pupils to the demands of a class or group programme more than is necessary to preserve good order and some kind of sequential progress; many believe that learning how to track down information, to study, to relate findings, and to present the finished product is more important than the exact subject matter chosen; and many are themselves experimentally minded and anxious to introduce new and contemporary material into the work of the school. Middle schools thus enjoy considerable curricular freedom, tempered, one might say, by their feeling of responsibility to their partners in the education service; but plainly to seek a common blueprint of curricular activity beyond the basic skills would be largely a waste of time. The pacemaker schools, and many others, are individual institutions with firm convictions and what they produce is different from that of their neighbours. There are of course some which remain on familiar tracks and do not seek new ways of learning or new curricular material; they are usually less interesting and less successful at stimulating initiative and resourceful habits of learning than are the others.

Although such wide differences of curricular cover will be found, individual schools are of course conscious of the main fields of human knowledge and the need to introduce pupils to them. In practice, no school is likely to ignore literature, the arts, science, crafts, history and a number of other curricular areas; but what they do under each heading may vary enormously. And the names of subjects on a time-table convey very little. To take a single example, all middle schools study some English literature; but so great is the wealth of prose, poetry, drama, fiction and non-fiction in our language that pupils in adjoining schools may all have read widely for four years and yet at the end of it have very few books in common. Ought there to be a common list? At first sight the argument may be attractive and yet it is difficult to arrive at a common choice and to prefer, for instance, Shakespeare to Dylan Thomas or Henry Treece to Jerome K. Jerome—

especially if teachers feel much more at home with one than with the other. The subject is quite a proper one for discussion in middle school and upper school circles; but in every branch of the curriculum the range of material is now so wide that to attempt to impose artificial limits on selection would certainly be strongly resisted by the best middle school teachers and would result in some impoverishment of courses.

Particular strengths of individual staffs are naturally a salient factor; the school which has on its staff a brilliant director of orchestral work or an expert in architecture or heraldry or continental cookery would be foolish not to make use of these talents. Schools which use their opportunities are therefore bound to be different. One other trend is the strong tendency to look at the whole curriculum in new ways and to integrate, or relate, whole areas of work under new generic titles—the humanities, environmental studies, the arts, social studies, and others. Each of these draws upon material from several of the old familiar 'subjects', to the extent that some of the old names (history and geography in particular) have often disappeared from time-tables altogether—though not from the actual work.

In a substantial number of middle schools work incorporating these trends is found. The variety is astonishing; the quality and often the depth of study and of presentation is very high indeed; the range of projects undertaken is remarkable; and performance in activities such as drama, music, art and crafts exceeds anything one would have seen involving pupils of these ages twenty years ago. In these schools a real tonic effect is evident which, if it flourishes and is transferable to others, cannot but benefit the whole of English education.

The curriculum is considered in more detail in the next chapter.

PART III

THE TOOLS FOR THE JOB

CHAPTER 9

Curriculum

Thought must start with the pupils themselves. And this
involves imagination as well as knowledge and experience.
(Raising the School Leaving Age;
Schools Council Working Paper No 2)

Shades of the prison-house begin to close
Upon the growing boy,
But he beholds the light, and whence it flows,
He sees it in his joy.
William Wordsworth
(Recollections of Early Childhood)

The curriculum is the daily bread of schools. It is the work
that is done, the material on which pupils sharpen their minds,
form their knowledge, awaken their imagination, develop
their personality. A school gets nowhere without it. A dull
curriculum produces lazy or apathetic children; a poorly
planned one leads to a hotch-potch of knowledge; a lively
and imaginative one encourages those qualities and attainments
which all good teachers seek to foster in their pupils. Was
Wordsworth being too visionary for real life? But it is the
school, the principal educative agency in the experience of
most children, that can illuminate their progress—as more than
a century later we find acknowledged in a very down to earth
Schools Council paper concerned with the world of to-day.

The curriculum cannot stand still except to the detriment
of those being educated. The world is changing; the sum of
human knowledge is changing; attitudes and life styles are
changing—and responsible teachers do not wish to enclose
either themselves or their pupils in an ivory tower. In the

previous chapter, in assessing the achievement so far of middle schools, we paid close attention to the basic skills as the groundwork of knowledge. Groundwork is of course essential; but it is not an end in itself, it is there so that a superstructure may be erected upon it, and in this case the superstructure is one of knowledge, abilities, and understanding of the world. This is worth emphasising because at present a widespread debate on the school curriculum is taking place, encouraged by such eminent persons as the Prime Minister and the Secretary of State for Education; and the debate undoubtedly reflects some anxiety in industry and among parents about the value of what the schools are actually achieving. Some people are tempted to believe that basic skills are all that matters, and that if the broader curriculum and the enquiry methods common in schools to-day could be abandoned and a return made to the more formal methods and more limited curriculum of the past, all would be well. This is illusion; in a world in which calculators and computers have replaced long tots in ledgers, even the basic skills cannot wear the dress of a generation or two ago. More than this—in a world where a ceaseless flow of knowledge, of research, and of new discovery is available to anyone, child or adult, within reach of a television switch, it is unreal to think that the schools either could or should cut themselves off from this flow.

(i) General Principles

From the day more than twenty years ago when the first Russian Sputnik soared into space and administered a severe shock to the Western democracies who had till then believed themselves pre-eminent in scientific and technological development, there has been in the West a strong focus not only on research and technology at the adult level but also on curriculum development in schools, where the foundations are laid. The process must continue, for in this country, to name but one worrying feature, the lack of attraction which applied science and engineering exercise as careers for young people means that to scrutinise what the schools are doing, and why, is inevitable and right. Middle schools have their pupils in very formative years, and cannot be excluded from scrutiny. They would of course maintain that it is not their task to channel pupils towards particular careers, but rather to ensure that they have a wide band of educational experience which will later help them to make their own choices. It follows that the middle school curriculum must be broad, giving experience in the humanities, the arts, mathematics, the sciences and religious and moral education; and it must offer the individual child during his four year course the chance to try himself out in all of these and to discover what his talents, interests and weaknesses really are. To take a single example, if he has learned that he cannot live without music (many people cannot) or, alternatively, that he has not a note of music in his head, he will have made a useful discovery; but he will not have made it at all unless music has a serious place in the curriculum. The curriculum is there to serve the individual pupils, and cannot do this if it is reduced to the lowest common factor.

This is the first principle that probably all thinking middle school staffs accept (though they would not necessarily place it first). The second is that the old subject divisions are, to some extent at least, unreal to middle school pupils—though as they mature they become more able to see individual sectors of knowledge not as something isolated but as part of a whole. When a group of children, under the guidance of a teacher or a team, look at their home town, they do not confine themselves to examining its geography, or its history, or its industries, or its leisure pursuits, or its government and social services separately and in isolation. In walking down a main street they have before them examples of town planning, engineering, architecture, merchandise from various sources, people at their daily occupations. If they cannot read, or cannot understand the language they hear, they are at a disadvantage; so the basic skills are present too. Many subjects will be combined by a special stimulus in this way,

though not to the exclusion of separate study; there will still
be specific language, mathematics, science or history teaching
in addition. Studies of this linked kind are however often
an important part of the curriculum. What they emphasise is
that knowledge is not fragmented, but that different branches
of it relate to each other. One major outcome has been the
deliberate planning in many schools of *integrated studies*
courses which draw upon several subject areas, and may
replace some of the old familiar subject names on the time-
tables. (History and geography are quite often absorbed in
this way, and other subjects may be too, according to the
actual standpoint of the school in curricular matters.)

The third general principle is that liberal attitudes to the
selection of subject matter are necessary, and that the actual
impact on the pupils of the selected matter needs to be carefully
observed and evaluated. What succeeded last year will not
necessarily do so next; the current interests of the pupils,
topical news, and the like affect the choice. In the early 1970s
space travel and landings on the moon sparked off a great
interest in astronomy, cosmology and the technical aspects of
space travel; in 1977, the year of the Queen's Silver Jubilee,
studies of the monarchy, its history, rôle and future are much
more commonly centres of interest. Schools seek a balance
in their curriculum between events which may fire the imagination, and those permanent areas of knowledge which underlie
so much of life that they cannot be ignored; much of science,
the laws of which do not change, and of mathematics come
under this last heading.

(ii) *A permanent core of knowledge?*

Most teachers would probably agree that there is a permanent
core of knowledge and of skills which all normal children
should be taught. But what is it? There has been little debate
on this question and there is no certainty about the answers.
It is easy to agree that all children should be able to read,
write and express themselves in speech, but what beyond that?

(Even this simple statement needs further definition; many eight year old children, and some a good deal younger, would be able mechanically to read the leaders and company reports in the *Financial Times,* but precisely how useful is this until they have studied the financial structures involved—an unlikely subject of study for an average eight year old?) Twenty-five years ago one could travel through junior schools and find almost identical syllabuses in school after school. In history, for instance, few apparently doubted that a straightforward chronological study, lasting four years, of British history from Julius Caesar's invasion to some point in the twentieth century (how recent depended on the nerve of the staff concerned) was good core historical study; to-day in the middle schools few teachers see any automatic virtue in the chronological sequence, but look instead for periods of history, not necessarily British, which catch the imagination and which illustrate human progress in differing forms, or which pose fundamental social questions which the teacher thinks it would be good for the pupils to discuss. And history is far from being the only subject in which the certainty of what constitutes essential knowledge has vanished.

Even where certainty remains, choice may still be bewildering. No-one doubts the value of studying English literature; and twenty-five years ago one could have made a good guess at three-quarters of the syllabus in three-quarters of the junior schools (some Dickens, Henty, Louisa Alcott, Walter Scott, Kenneth Grahame, A. A. Milne, some anthologies of short stories and of mainly Victorian lyric poetry, perhaps a little Shakespeare). To-day schools choose from the vast range of English writing, past and present; they buy books in ones and twos, no longer in class sets, and pupils are encouraged to read widely and to comment on what they have read. Is it better to have read W. H. G. Kingston or Henry Treece? Wordsworth or Walter de la Mare? The choice will in fact be local, made for particular reasons in the individual school— and a further characteristic of the middle school curriculum is therefore the diversity of its subject matter.

But it would be wrong to think there is no common ground; there are unifying factors also. The composite schools studied in Chapter 6 do give a fair illustration of the range of different approaches; but within the same locality there may often be similarities. Local consultation and local in-service training are certainly not without influence; many teachers formed the habit of joint planning when preparing in their area for reorganisation and have continued it since. Some schools have participated in field trials of the curriculum development projects sponsored by the Schools Council and many make use of the materials and publications of this national body. There have been a number of courses and conferences run by HM Inspectorate, university institutes or departments of education and other bodies which are valuable forums for exchanging information and experiences; one of these, arranged in 1975 by the University of Bradford Post-graduate School in Research in Education, drew members from middle schools throughout the country and led to the establishment of follow-up groups to explore curricular issues throughout the following winter.

One further factor is that several of the 9 to 13 schools have firm roots in secondary education in that their heads, many of their staff, and their buildings came from that sector. They are perhaps particularly aware of the desirability of depth studies towards the end of their courses and of laying good general foundations of knowledge in many areas of the curriculum. In the developmental subjects such as foreign languages and mathematics, teaching methods can be varied but subject matter does have to follow certain sequences or the links essential to mastering them just are not there. Many of these schools do in fact blend the best of primary and secondary practices, producing a curriculum which progresses from wide ranging exploratory approaches in the early years to more continuous studies in the later years and which is related both to what precedes them and to what may follow them in the upper schools.

(iii) New Approaches to the Curriculum

We have identified three widely accepted principles: that the curriculum must be broad, that there must be a measure of integration of subjects or at least of inter-relationship between them, and that there must be a liberal attitude to the selection of material from the great store of knowledge now at our fingers' ends—this last qualified by the need to prepare the pupils for an easy transition to the next stage of their education.

SOME EARLY THINKING

The most important general approach to emerge from these is the tendency to look at the curriculum in broad areas instead of in subjects. There are several ways of doing this. An early one given as an example in *Towards the Middle School* contained four broad groups: *language,* which included all work in both English and the foreign language studied, usually French; *social studies,* which drew upon history, geography and facets of society past and present; *science and mathematics,* linked partly because many teachers would be competent in both, and the *aesthetic group* consisting of the arts and crafts, music and movement. This grouping leans strongly towards primary practice, and the notable omissions from it, such as religious education and physical education other than the imaginative forms described technically as *movement,* show that the exercise is not easy. A second suggested triple grouping in the same pamphlet consisted of: *the humanities,* ie all those subjects which focus upon man, his achievements, and his values (literature, religious education, history, human geography and some forms of art); *environmental study,* encompassing science, some geography and history, and making use of mathematics, art and language as tools; and *the visual and tactile arts and crafts* in their own right, including handicraft, needlecraft and home economics. This grouping, like many, left some aspects of the curriculum unaccounted for, including the foreign language, music, physical education and the sequential work in mathematics. It is far more difficult than it appears to establish a few broad groupings which take in the whole of the curricular work of the school, and versions adopted in schools since then have usually solved this problem by adopting more groups than these or by not being afraid to leave one or two subjects outside them and treating them on their own.

If the question is asked whether the exercise is worth while, the answer is that it has certainly proved so. Not only does it correspond to some of the curricular realities we have outlined, but it brings staff together in groups to discuss and work out the inter-relationship of subjects; and it enables senior posts to be created with responsibility for the general strategy and oversight of all the work taking place within that curricular grouping. Most members of a middle school staff will be involved in more than one group, but the oversight of each can be given to some-one with the time, the experience, and the responsibility to see it as a whole and to offer help. It means also that the head and these few senior teachers can together compose a curricular steering group which is in more or less continuous session and which can also undertake the task of evaluation.

A curricular network of this kind is by no means incompatible with another grouping of staff much favoured by larger middle schools, namely the year group. In this all the teachers working in a particular year form a team, again under the leadership of a senior teacher responsible for the oversight of all the work and all the pupils' progress in the year. Most teachers will again be involved in the work of more than one year group. The two networks can be beneficially complementary, and certainly in organisational patterns such as these no teacher is left out in the cold; all have a many sided view of what is going on. They also provide reassurance that important learning skills and attitudes are being practised by pupils in several different contexts. To quote again from *Towards the Middle School:* 'Some objectives can be readily identified with the aims of certain aspects of the curriculum, or indeed more narrowly with those of subjects. But many concepts, skills and attitudes can be fostered through several elements of the traditional curriculum'—and how much more effectively when within such groupings varying opportunities can arise!

It is clear from discussions within schools that the period of experiment is not over; most still view their individual curriculum groupings as tentative and liable to change. The approach though by no means universal (and it is in any case most often found in the larger schools) is widespread enough to make one think it has come to stay; and flexibility is after all the essence of it. Three current examples may each indicate some differences in thought about groupings.

The first, from an 8 to 12 school, sees the curriculum in four areas: *basic subjects,* ie speaking, reading, writing, spelling and mathematics; *activities in exploration,* ie history, geography, nature study and general science; *physical activities,* ie physical training, games, dancing and swimming; and *creative activities,* ie music, acting, painting, needlework, craft, modelling and literature. These four headings and the activities which make them up are in line with the main primary trends; some of the doubters about these trends may be reassured to see how firmly basic subjects remain in the school's thinking, even to the special mention of spelling. Something can be deduced about the approach to science from its position, an enquiry based subject, and about the importance given to a wide experience of creative activities. What does not appear from this curricular analysis is that religious education and French also receive serious attention in the school in question, that music is outstanding with two school orchestras and every child taught at least recorder and percussion, that drama is equally flourishing and acts not only as an outlet for all children but as a focus for scenery design, costuming, dancing, play and song writing in addition to acting, and that a great deal of the school's work is centred upon projects which draw upon and reinforce many areas of the curriculum.

The other two examples are from 9 to 13 schools. The first relies on what is basically a secondary type of organisation, with subject teams for *foreign languages* (French and probably a second to follow), *environmental studies, art and craft,* and *mathematics and science. Integrated studies* are however of major importance alongside these groups; and a curricular balance is sought in each year's work by undertaking integrated studies which draw upon the humanities, religious education, environmental studies, geography and history. The second considers no fewer than seven groups to be necessary; and in this case less use is made of projects and integrated studies. The seven groups are *languages* (reading, English, French and Latin—the last-named a very unusual middle school subject, but one challenging to able pupils), *mathematics, science* (including rural science), *environmental studies, art, craft and design* (including housecraft), *music and physical education* (including movement and drama), and *religious education with assembly.*

(iv) New sources of curricular material

The same period of time that has seen the development and translation into action of the middle school idea has seen the most vigorous and varied curriculum development this country has known. If reaction to the Sputnik on this side of the Atlantic was less sharp than in North America, there was nevertheless concern in high places that Britain should not fall behind in educational advance. For this and other reasons, the Ministry of Education set up in 1963 an internal curriculum study group, soon to be absorbed into the much larger Schools Council, which in a somewhat controversial career has nevertheless established itself as a major and valuable influence. Its full title is *The Schools Council for the Curriculum and Examinations;* our concern is with the first of these two responsibilities. In this field it is an agency for curriculum development and research, funded jointly by the DES and the local education authorities, staffed mainly by professionals on short-term release from their schools or other institutions, and having major teacher representation on all its main committees. In the fourteen years since it was set up, it has undertaken development projects across most of the curriculum, has engaged schools throughout the country as participants in them, has published reports, produced materials, and set up a network of field officers who can visit schools and co-operate with local in-service training agencies, organise local conferences, and so on. The specific materials developed in many projects such as *Science 5–13, History, Geography and Social Science 8–13* and *English for Immigrant Children 5–16+* bring valuable reinforcement to the classroom in the shape of units which children can work through and which are in general based on enlivening enquiry techniques; even so, to some teachers the new lines of teaching suggested in the reports and publications are equally useful as starters for new curricular programmes.

The Council has looked generally at overlapping age ranges; its main committees deal with education from 3 to 13, 11 to 16, and 13 to 18 respectively. Projects may deal with any useful age range; the examples above illustrate this. Though the Council does not gear them to particular types of school, projects such as the one in *history, geography and social science* quoted above are tailor-made for the middle school, while *Science 5–13* furnishes for it a great deal of directly usable or easily adaptable material. The list of projects which middle schools can use, in whole or in part, is too long to quote here (though some of the more widely used are listed in Appendix B). In addition to projects producing materials for branches of the curriculum, there have been two reports from the project *The Curriculum in the Middle Years* (1972 and 1976) based at the University of Lancaster under the direction of Professor Alec Ross.

The work of the Schools Council has been accompanied by the growth of *local in-service training* on a remarkable scale.

There are now some hundreds of teachers' centres in the country, of differing size, purpose and constitution. Without them the activity in many areas during the peiord of preparation for the setting up of middle schools would have been impossible. Teachers met in them in inter-school and inter-curricular groups, single subject groups, and in further education classes to improve their ability to teach certain subjects or to take them at a higher level. Most centres are run, or funded, by local education authorities; but university departments of education, colleges of education, and teachers' associations also play a helpful part. Some middle school teachers also follow Open University courses. Altogether, sources of help in the curricular field are now many and various, and indeed some teachers will say that what they most need is a period in which to digest all that is available. Local education authorities too have built up their own staffs of advisers who keep in touch with the schools and whose services in some places are in such demand that they cannot meet all the calls made upon them. There is certainly no likelihood of curriculum development in the middle schools coming to a halt for lack either of enthusiasm in the schools themselves or of supporting services.

Perhaps the most significant feature of all is the zest with which teachers themselves have helped to generate these new approaches and materials. If what they require is not readily available from educational publishers or suppliers, it is likely to be produced by themselves in their own schools, in teachers' centres, or in workshops in other educational institutions. So long as this continues, the curriculum will remain dynamic and will respond to developments in society as well as in the classroom.

(v) School Organisation; its function

It is difficult to say quite how widely accepted are the principles and practices described in this chapter. Certainly a substantial number of schools subscribe to them—especially those in areas where there has long been lively educational thinking, in areas where middle schools have been well prepared and planned, and in schools favoured by both staffing and material resources. In contrast, there are undoubtedly some areas where the run-up to middle schools was too rapid for proper thought and planning at school level, where material provision too much resembles the former junior school under a new name, and where the number of small schools has much restricted the possibilities of curricular advance. The country's economic difficulties, inevitably bringing some restrictions on educational finance, cannot fail to impose some sort of a halt on material provision; and some authorities are having to postpone either the implementation of particular re-organisation plans or the envisaged provision of additional resources for individual schools. Financial restrictions need not, of course, impose a check on educational thinking; but it is sad that already economies have forced the abandonment of at least one major middle schools curricular conference which had been arranged at Bradford for the autumn of 1976 as a follow-up to the work of curricular study groups.

School organisation is the instrument for applying the school's ideas and achieving its aims; its function is to make the best use of human and material resources. Many of the approaches and methods described in Chapter 6 and in this chapter, particularly those involving integrated study teams and the scheduling of work with small groups or with individual children, call for considerable organisational skill in such matters as the deployment of staff and the mechanics of time-tabling. It is inescapable that the larger school has opportunities for offering more curricular choice and more varied ways of implementing the wishes of staff and pupils than has the small school. The latter has less room for manoeuvre, has a narrower range of talent to draw on, and is more vulnerable to illness or other interruptions.

It is not the intention in this study to enter into the often complex details of organising the large school to the best advantage. This has been admirably done by two experienced and perceptive headmasters in a recent book in which principles of management, curricular options, and systems of internal organisation are carefully analyzed and which readers concerned with these aspects are advised to consult *(Middle Schools,* by Gannon and Whalley, 1976).

CHAPTER 10

Buildings and Resources

The classroom as we remember it represents architectural perfection for a mode of education which even to-day's more formal primary teachers would reject out of hand . . . . The move away from the box-like classroom was not caused by bright young architects who wanted to experiment. It was caused by pressure from teachers demanding better facilities for the children with and for whom they worked.

Henry Pluckrose,
(Open School, Open Society)

In the above words Henry Pluckrose, a thoughtful and experimentally minded primary headmaster, emphasises the importance of the partnership between the architect and his design team on the one hand and teachers on the other—with, of course, the essential links provided by understanding administrators. So much depends on the design of school buildings; but the architect can design only in accordance with the details of the educational brief which he receives. If this tells him little more than the numbers and age range of the pupils for whom the school is to be built, the cost limits and DES regulations about minimum teaching areas, lighting standards and so on, he is not likely to produce other than a workaday and unimspired building—certainly nothing like the imaginative designs described in earlier chapters. He needs to understand the philosophy, the aims and likely characteristics of the kind of school he is to design — what the teachers wish to achieve and what kind of facilities they would like to have to do so.

In fact, to write an educational brief in terms which a design team can interpret and translate into buildings is by no means easy, and it is noteworthy that the areas where the most successful buildings have been produced are those where architects have themselves visited schools to see teachers' ideas being put into practice and to hear from them how their present buildings help or hinder them. Such an approach is almost always supported by continuing discussions throughout the design stages, involving architects, educational advisers and teachers, administrators, supplies officers, and others. The method is time-consuming and can of course only be applied to key schools where new ground is to be broken in educational and design terms; but the experience of this first thorough approach can relatively easily be transferred to subsequent designs based on similar briefs, and the feedback of information from newly opened schools adds practical experience to the team's knowledge.

The ideal situation is one in which a new school is to be designed from the very beginning to meet clear educational requirements. The first middle schools often presented this opportunity. A choice had to be made, clear and definite, about aims and working approaches; and, since several different approaches were possible, designs had to be as adaptable as possible in case the aims and approaches in question were later found to need modification in practice. Once the principles on which a new school was to be designed were established in an area or by a particular team, schemes for the extension or adaptation of existing schools became a challenge to apply as much of the new thinking as was practicable to them also. We therefore examine the needs which most of the pioneer authorities have identified as the basis for their new school designs.

General Criteria

Good designs meet three criteria. They respond to current educational and social needs within the school community;

they try to foresee likely changes in curriculum and method, instead of designing for the practices of yesterday; and either alternative methods are possible within them or structural adaptations would be reasonably easy to make if desired later on – in contrast to the solidly built schools of the Victorian era!

Basic Working Spaces

The enclosed rectangular classroom, as Henry Pluckrose implied, has very limited forms of use. To-day's approaches to teaching and learning call for easy movement by both teachers and pupils, facilities for active physical pursuits, provision both for quiet study and for noisy practical occupations, easy handling by pupils of small apparatus and resources, and large-scale displays of finished or part-complete projects and other forms of work. The multiplication of approaches, in contrast to the 'chalk and talk' techniques and sitting at the desk of earlier generations, has led designers to aim at multi-purpose spaces which, with the aid of light mobile furniture, portable or folding screens, and other devices, can be rapidly divided, enlarged, or otherwise transformed. In many of these schools any need can thus be met, from the individual or small group tutorial to the talk, concert, play or film which brings together a team of teachers and a hundred or more pupils.

These basic working spaces are often so designed as to give interesting views as pupils move around a wing or make their way through a series of communicating rooms. Some may be equipped with large flat working surfaces, tiled flooring, and water and electric points so that a variety of practical crafts can take place in them; others may be curtained and carpeted for teachers to gather their own class together for direct teaching in quiet comfort. In these basic working spaces it is usually easy for schools to organise reading and writing tables, library and music corners, mathematics and nature study bays, and others besides. This kind of provision is congenial to the 8 to 12 school in particular; in the 9 to 13 school it also has its place but more specialised accommodation is usually found as well.

Specialised Accommodation

There are alternative approaches to many of the subjects which need a measure of specialist accommodation—science, practical crafts, or physical education. Both effective teaching and safety precautions may favour single-purpose spaces for science and for crafts such as wood and metal work. In new schools both forms of provision may however be found; some schools have open craft areas equipped with services, benches, and a minimum of fixed apparatus, while others have specially designed enclosed laboratories or workshops, sometimes located so that combined projects with related subjects are relatively easy to organise. In adapted buildings of former secondary schools it is the latter which is general, though sometimes access to other rooms for related work has been improved and fixed heavy benches may have been replaced by lighter, more manageable furniture. Local interests are often acknowledged— for instance, rooms specially designed for rural or environmental science are common in country schools. It has however been indicated earlier that in small 8 to 12 schools and in the even smaller *combined schools* several of these subjects may have to share facilities in a one or two room *conversion unit,* where compromise has to be the order of the day.

The relationship between accommodation and curricular development is a changing and an interesting one. In science, for instance, the Schools Council's carefully researched and detailed *Science 5–13* programmes have been adopted with enthusiasm by many schools; these are more topic-centred and less sequential than earlier traditional science teaching, drawing on examples of scientific study and method from a wide range of natural phenomena and human applications, and needing a flexible general purposes science workroom rather than a fixed-equipment laboratory. But the range of possible approaches to science teaching is so wide that no designer could meet them all, and accommodation adaptable to as many purposes as possible is what he often tries to provide.

The changing curriculum strongly influences current design, but what the designer ought to provide can involve difficult decisions. For instance, there is a strong trend towards giving girls and boys equal experience of manual and domestic crafts such as wood and metal work, cookery and household management; but school accommodation in the past was usually provided on the assumption that these crafts were for a single sex only, and more space and more facilities are now needed for both. In a rather different way, the demands of art education are also increasing; art was never confined to a single sex, but its range is widening to include many two and three dimensional skills, painting, modelling, collage, the artistic use of fabrics, pottery with its need for a specially paved and equipped working space and a kiln housing, weaving with space for looms, and so on—and all need storage on a far more generous scale than hitherto. Moreover, many schools now favour an integrated approach to the curriculum, and are discontented if the accommodation for each of these various branches of the curriculum is shut away and self-contained. Architects and their teams often try therefore to group the accommodation for a considerable range of specialised activities together, seeking reasonable proximity in a way that can be combined with economy in the provision of services. This is more easily done in square rather than linear blocks or wings, and the design of many new middle schools shows this. Enthusiasts could well make a case for special accommodation for other areas of the curriculum—social studies, a foreign language, religious education; and indeed all have new needs as a result of new teaching methods and greatly expanded resources. But compromise there has to be, since it is impossible within realistic cost limits to meet all such aspirations, except perhaps in the former secondary school building with its enclosed classrooms—and there it can only be at the expense of curricular integration. Meanwhile, the architect cannot wait until prevailing trends either become firmly established or fade away; he can at best so design as to leave the maximum number of working choices open to the staffs of the schools.

The larger the school, the greater is the number of different purposes which can be served. The school with fewer than 300 pupils fares poorly in regard to specialised accommodation, and has to put greater reliance on multi-purpose rooms and spaces. This is not necessarily unwelcome to schools which believe in an integrated approach, and the attractions of spaces which can be used in different ways is considerable. The various design plans which follow this chapter contain typical examples of certain spaces being designed and equipped to meet the requirements of a particular subject (Science, Music, Home Economics) while other spaces are not so designated and can be adapted to the use which the head and staff wish to make of them at any given time.

Other Spaces

The most costly single space in any school is the hall, and its use cannot be restricted to corporate assemblies and acts of worship, important to school life as these are. Most middle schools use the hall also for physical education, dance, drama, and some musical activities; in many schools it is valuable after school hours for parents' gatherings and community functions also. Some of these uses have their own special requirements; dance and drama need mainly uncluttered space, and are easier in a square rather than a rectangular shape. Music needs certain acoustic properties. Gymnastics may need some fixed and some portable apparatus. All of these will need adjacent storage for their equipment. In some schools too the hall will have to be used for school meals, and accessibility to the kitchen is important. All in all, the hall can present the architect with quite a batch of problems; the remarkable fact is that so many successfully meet such a variety of uses. Larger schools may have a separate dining hall, and some architects have enhanced its usefulness by placing it next to the main hall (sometimes on a slightly different level) and considerably extending the joint range of uses.

The range of musical education to-day is too wide to be met solely in a hall, which is in any case often unsuitable for quiet listening and for much instrumental work; some additional facilities are needed. A good design facilitates singing, listening, appreciation, composing, and instrumental work with a variety of instruments in groups both small and large; some small practice rooms are almost essential. Visual aids is another field where normally a special room is necessary in addition to whatever may be possible in normal working spaces; the teaching of French through audio-visual courses, for instance, needs in fairness to other activities to be in a sound-proof room. Library needs have also to be met, and, though there should be ready provision of books wherever learning is going on, every middle school of any size needs a central library or a series of sectional libraries in addition, both for reference and for quiet study.

The design and location of administrative rooms, cloak-rooms and other ancillary accommodation can occupy design teams for a long time; but the one additional point to be made here is that the school needs to be welcoming to visitors from the local community, especially parents, and that the design of its buildings should contribute to this. The entrance foyer, imaginatively designed, can be an asset; and a few recently built schools have even included a parents' common room where they are encouraged to come and meet staff and each other.

Furnishings and Equipment

In the last twenty-five years or so the Architects and Buildings Branch of the DES has rendered a valuable service not only in relating the design of buildings to educational needs but also in regarding materials, furnishings and equipment as an integral part of the whole design. It is important to select furnishings such as carpets and curtains with an eye to the visual and acoustic properties of the building itself; this is not only a matter of appearance but of suitability. Carpets and curtains will absorb sound very effectively if correctly chosen and placed, and thereby increase the ease of working within the school; perhaps 'correctly' should be emphasised, for it has been known for a well intentioned supplies officer to carpet even the tiled area within a pottery bay, with disastrous results when the time came to clean up the inevitable wet clay. The choice of flooring for different rooms should similarly be related to their use, and there has been much progress in testing and marketing suitable ranges.

Among other advances, one of the most welcome has been the introduction of light stackable furniture, enabling teachers to change class activities quickly from sedentary to active pursuits. Lockers for children's personal effects, bookcases, storage cupboards, and display screens can be mounted on wheels or castors and similarly be easily moved at will. A useful by-product of open-plan designs, which allows many activities to be pursued by pupils at the same time, is that fewer chairs and tables are needed as compared with older methods of teaching; where group activities are in use, it rarely happens that every child needs a chair or working surface at the same time.

In the field of teaching equipment, much use is made of the kind of lightweight portable aids which to-day children confidently use on their own; film loops and viewers, playback recorders, hand-held cameras; there is less need for the bulky and heavy equipment of the past. The kind of machines and apparatus installed in handicraft, housecraft, and science rooms varies according to the age range of the school and its curricular policy. In many 9 to 13 schools it includes quite a full range of wood and metal work apparatus, of sewing machines, cookers and other domestic equipment, a range of laboratory equipment for science, and for art maybe a potter's wheel, a kiln, and weaving machines. Much of this is expensive, and it is not found in all schools, some considering that sophisticated machines should be left to the next stage of education.

Books are of course a major tool of learning, and rising prices are an increasing worry. Some new middle schools opened with inadequate resources, and though help is often obtainable from local authority school library services, this is never the same as having one's own books on tap when and where they are needed—which means adequate accommodation for books as well as the books themselves. Many local authorities have built up school museum services which offer loan collections; such resources usefully supplement a school's own, but outside sources are under heavy pressure and the loss to schools will be considerable if they have neither the funds nor the space to build up their own.

Outdoor Facilities

As with the buildings themselves, the DES prescribes minimum site sizes for new schools according to the number and age range of pupils. This normally includes a minimum area of hard playing space; beyond this, it is for the authority and its designers to determine the use and lay-out of the site. The obvious curricular needs to be served are the common sports and team games appropriate to the age range, usually football and cricket for the boys, netball, shinty and rounders for the girls, athletics and perhaps hockey and basketball for both. Some schools introduce other games, too; rugby football and baseball are to be found, though rarely. Tennis has grown in popularity for both sexes and of course requires either hard or grass courts according to the funds available or the optimism of the local weather forecasters. For some of these games hard playing space is more serviceable, being less affected by weather conditions, than grass; but it is more expensive to provide and leaves less funds for other purposes. Athletics, besides being popular, fortunately requires relatively little site expenditure.

This does not exhaust the possibilities. Swimming as both sport and pastime is very popular and, on safety grounds too, a useful skill for children to acquire. Some authorities consider it worthwhile to economise on some of the other facilities in order to provide a swimming pool, either open and outdoors or, less frequently, covered and heated and so usable all the year round. Only the largest middle schools can aspire to a heated pool; but there are one or two cases where a pool is shared with other schools and the cost of heating covered.

Well laid out grounds are both pleasant and useful. The obsession which at one time appeared to afflict design teams that all outside space must be flat has happily disappeared (in most areas at least), and where contours lend themselves to it the grounds around some schools have been attractively landscaped. Flower borders, garden pool and rockeries can provide observation and study material for biology and environmental science programmes as well as being pleasant to look at. An even happier example was the school described in Chapter 6 as having its own nature reserve within the grounds; this reference was based on one where the site included on purchase the small copse on a chalk slope complete with flora and fauna. The design team saw its educational value and left it intact to form a distinctive element in the environmental studies course. Dance and drama are two other activities which, given the right setting, can take place out of doors; and in one or two places a little simple landscaping has created the effect of a classical amphitheatre in miniature.

Recent developments, in fact, have seen in school grounds both a thoroughly useful curricular resource and an attractive setting for the school.

The Present Position

Only a small proportion of the more than 1500 middle schools enjoy new purpose designed buildings. The principles underlying these designs—and the numbers of local education authorities involved have ensured a wide variety—have however also been widely applied, so far as was possible, to the adaptation or extension of older buildings for middle school use.

In many, perhaps, most, of the purpose built schools the year group has been taken as the natural planning unit and the design based on four such wings, differently planned for the needs of the different ages, housed around a central nucleus of other accommodation. Specialist facilities are often located in or adjoining these year centres or wings, but not always; sometimes they are designed as the main centres themselves, particularly where the design has looked to the best in secondary building design. Single-storey design has generally been favoured for 8 to 12, and for some 9 to 13, schools; but some architects have considered two-storey buildings valuable since they take up less of the available ground area and release more for the outdoor activities.

Most of the new designs in effect invite staffs to try out new modes of working, frequently based on forms of team or co-operative teaching; and many staffs are constantly evaluating their own performance. In a few years from now a study of the most effective approaches and their relationship to buildings and resources will be valuable; meanwhile, there is constant interplay between the two and school design will continue to evolve. The selection of design plans of actual schools reproduced on pages 163 to 174 illustrates both some of the commoner types and the development which has taken place in less than ten years. The earliest school illustrated was designed in 1966, the most recent in 1974; but a comparison of the various designs will show how, although the underlying principles of the designs have much in common (open circulation, association of different curricular areas, and the provision of adaptable multi-purpose spaces), designs have become more relaxed, the shapes and juxtaposition of working spaces more adventurous, and the whole building more versatile in use.

It has been said that the majority of middle schools are not purpose built but are former primary or secondary school buildings converted, adapted or extended. Clearly each single school has presented an individual problem; sometimes much was possible in the way of conversion or extension, sometimes little. It would be misleading to search for 'typical' examples and this has not been done. The two designs included which are not of purpose built schools (figs 9 and 10) are of one extremely successful conversion of a junior school where the original building lent itself to imaginative re-modelling, and of one prototype design of a small extension intended to add to existing facilities in former primary buildings. But observers must not be surprised if in many areas they find that premises of small middle schools especially show remarkably little change from their previous condition, and if in consequence the concept of education in the middle years which this book has tried to describe has made rather little headway. Though the finest buildings cannot positively guarantee a school where performance is outstanding, and though a staff with vision and determination will work wonders even in cramping premises, yet buildings can emphatically help or hinder—and even in a time of declining school rolls there is much that could be done to improve existing resources without major new building. This should not be forgotten in the years immediately ahead.

A. *Purpose built schools*

School	Age range	No. of pupils for which designed	Date
Fig. 1. Southampton, Townhill M.S.	8–12	480	1971
Fig. 2. Townhill M.S.—detail of Upper School Centre for 240 pupils			
Fig. 3. Buckinghamshire, Walters Ash M.S.	8–12	400	1972
Fig. 4. Walters Ash M.S.—detail of Centre 1 for 100 pupils			
Fig. 5. Bradford, Delf Hill M.S.	9–13	420	1966
Fig. 6. Delf Hill M.S.—detail of Year Centre 2 for 105 pupils			
Fig. 7. Service Children's Education Authority: prototype middle school for British Families Education Service, BAOR	9–13	540	1974

B. *Example of conversion of a junior school for age range 7–11 to a middle school for age range 8–12: 320 pupils, conversion 1972 (Buckinghamshire, Woodside School, Amersham)*

Fig. 8. Original Woodside Junior School

Fig. 9. As converted to Woodside Middle School

C. *Prototype conversion unit to provide accommodation for workshop and domestic crafts; to extend facilities at junior or primary schools having to serve as middle schools.*

Fig. 10. Conversion unit: plan taken from Building Bulletin No. 35, HMSO. (Examples of similar units for other curricular purposes may be found in the same Bulletin.)

Fig. 1

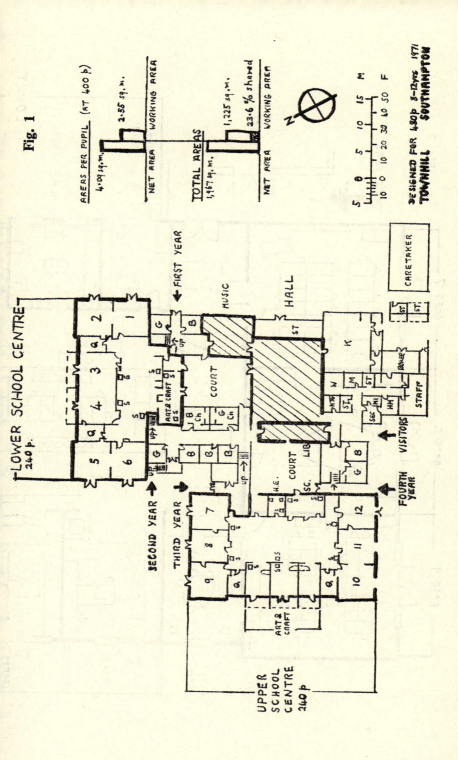

AREAS PER PUPIL (AT 400 p)

4·09 sq.m. — NET AREA

2·56 sq.m. — WORKING AREA

TOTAL AREAS

1,167 sq.m. — NET AREA

1,225 sq.m. — WORKING AREA

23·6 % shared

DESIGNED FOR 480p 8–12 yrs 1971
TOWNHILL SOUTHAMPTON

LOWER SCHOOL CENTRE 240 p.

FIRST YEAR

SECOND YEAR

THIRD YEAR

FOURTH YEAR

UPPER SCHOOL CENTRE 240 p.

MUSIC

HALL

COURT

COURT

LIB.

CARETAKER

VISITORS

ART & CRAFT

ART & CRAFT

H.E.

STAFF

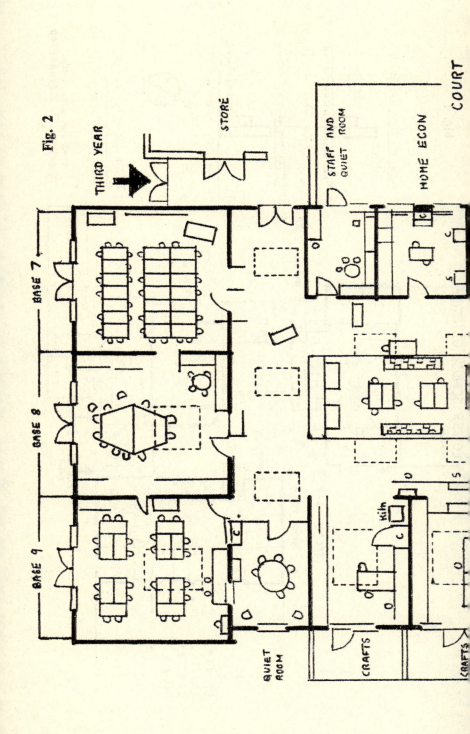

Fig. 2

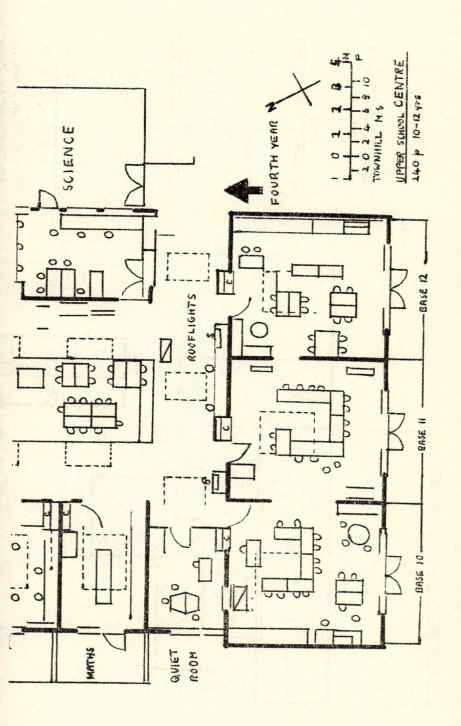

SCIENCE

MATHS

QUIET
ROOM

ROOFLIGHTS

FOURTH YEAR

BASE 10   BASE 11   BASE 12

TOWNHILL M S

UPPER SCHOOL CENTRE
140 p 10-12 yrs

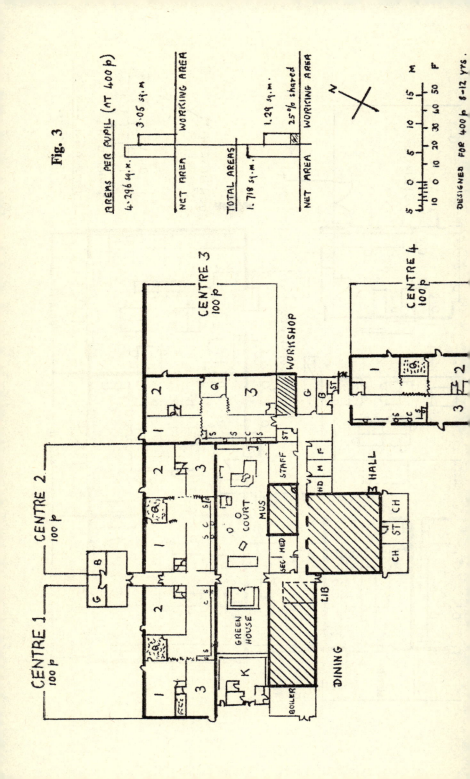

Fig. 3

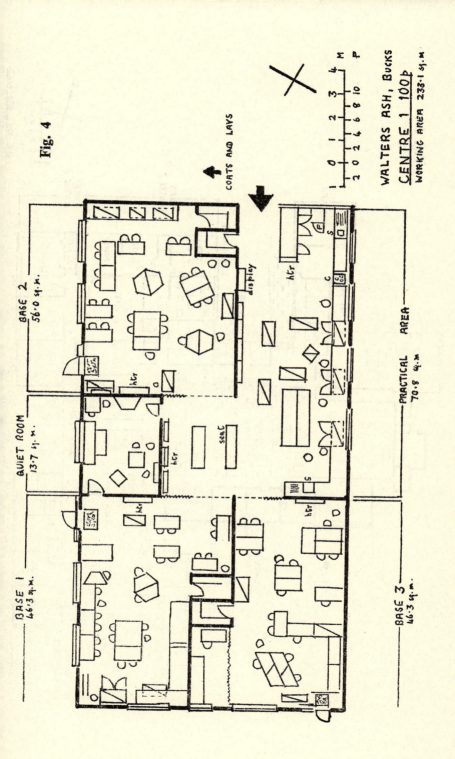

Fig. 4

BASE 2
56·0 sq.m.

QUIET ROOM
13·7 sq.m.

BASE 1
46·3 sq.m.

BASE 3
46·3 sq.m.

COATS AND LAVS

display

seat

htr

PRACTICAL AREA
70·8 sq.m.

WALTERS ASH, BUCKS
CENTRE 1 100p
WORKING AREA 233·1 sq.m.

Fig. 5

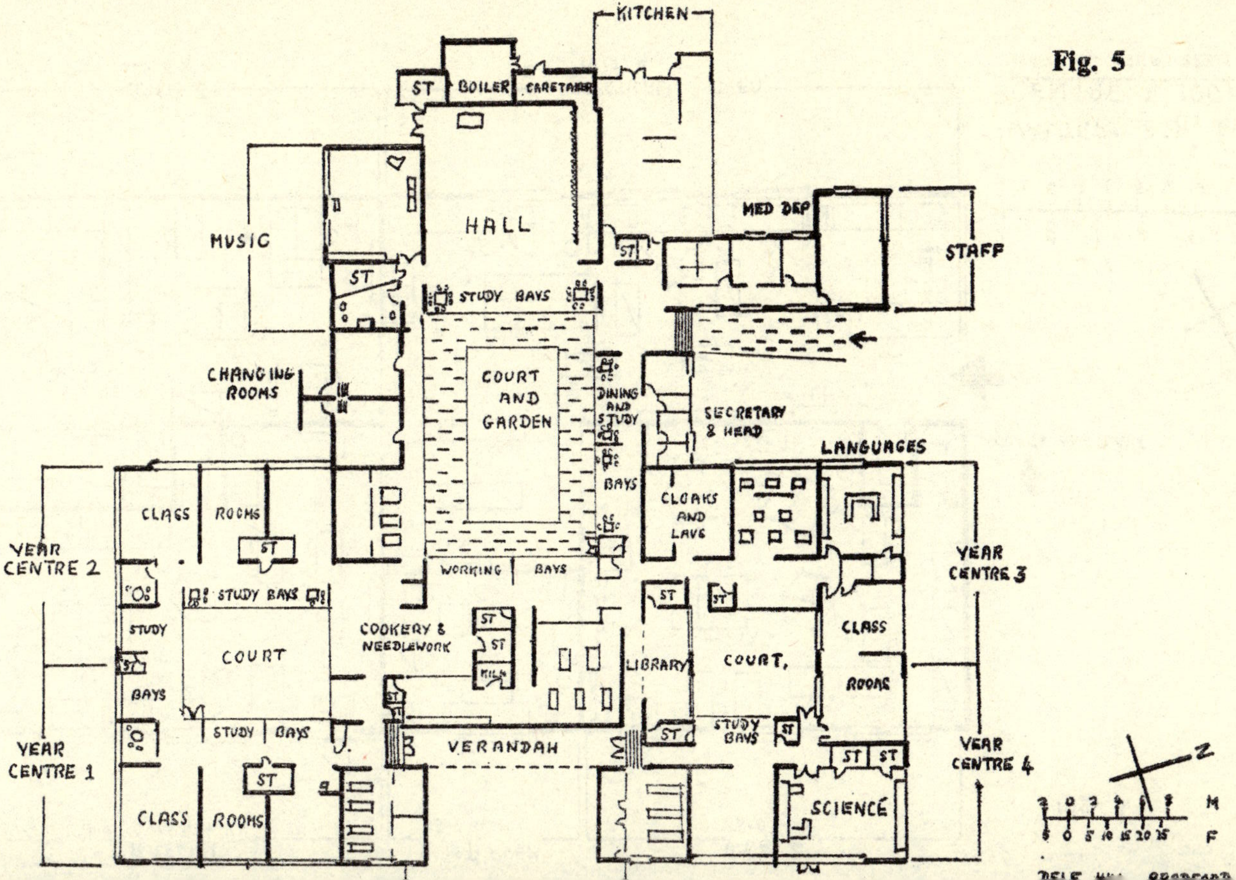
KITCHEN
ST
BOILER
CARETAKER
HALL
MUSIC
ST
STUDY BAYS
MED DEP
ST
STAFF
CHANGING ROOMS
COURT AND GARDEN
DINING AND STUDY
BAYS
SECRETARY & HEAD
LANGUAGES
CLOAKS AND LAVS
CLASS
ROOMS
ST
YEAR CENTRE 2
STUDY BAYS
WORKING BAYS
YEAR CENTRE 3
STUDY
COURT
COOKERY & NEEDLEWORK
ST
ST
KILN
LIBRARY
COURT
CLASS
ROOMS
BAYS
STUDY BAYS
STUDY BAYS
YEAR CENTRE 1
VERANDAH
YEAR CENTRE 4
ST
ST
ST
CLASS
ROOMS
SCIENCE
N
M
F

Fig. 6

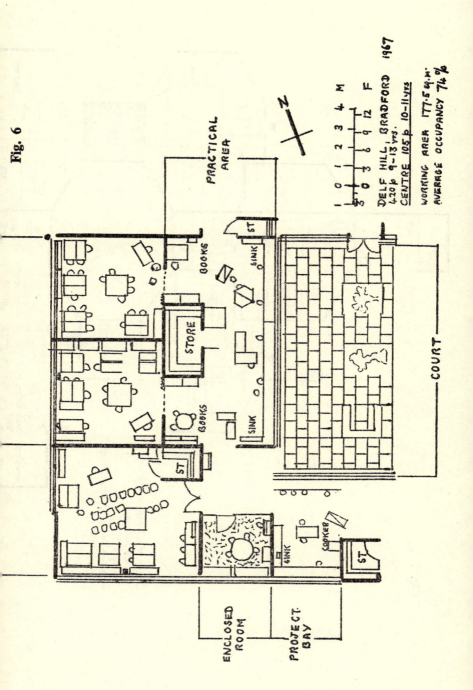

PRACTICAL AREA

DELF HILL, BRADFORD 1967
420 b 9-13 yrs.
CENTRE 105 b 10-11yrs

WORKING AREA 177·5 sq.m.
AVERAGE OCCUPANCY 74%

BOOKS

ST

SINK

STORE

BOOKS

SINK

ST

COURT

SINK

COOKER

ST

ENCLOSED ROOM

PROJECT BAY

M

Fig. 7

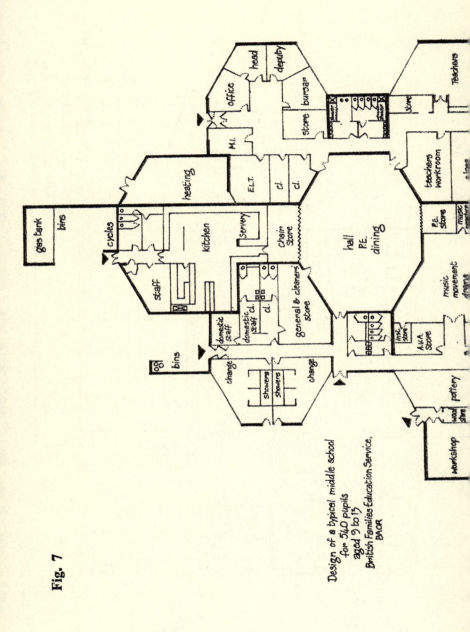

Design of a typical middle school
for 540 pupils
aged 9 to 13
British Families Education Service,
BAOR

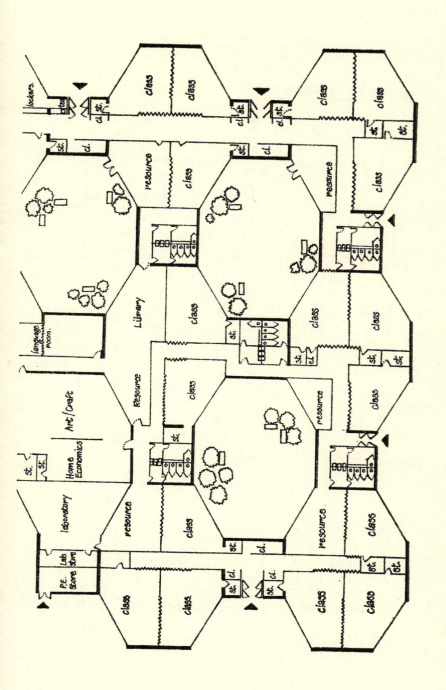

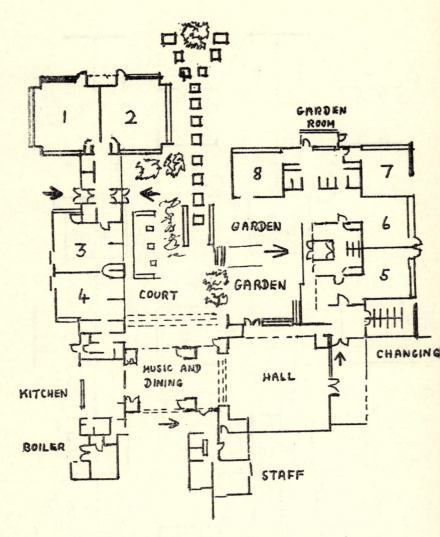

WOODSIDE JUNIOR SCHOOL
AMERSHAM, BUCKS

DESIGNED FOR 320 PUPILS AGED 7-11 YEARS
1955

Fig. 8

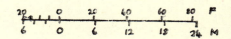

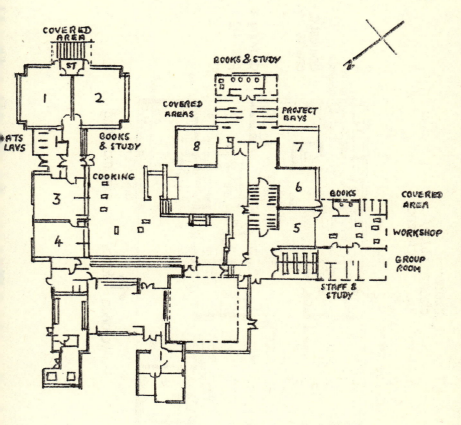

WOODSIDE MIDDLE SCHOOL

CONVERTED FOR 320 PUPILS AGED 8-13 YEARS
1972

Fig. 9

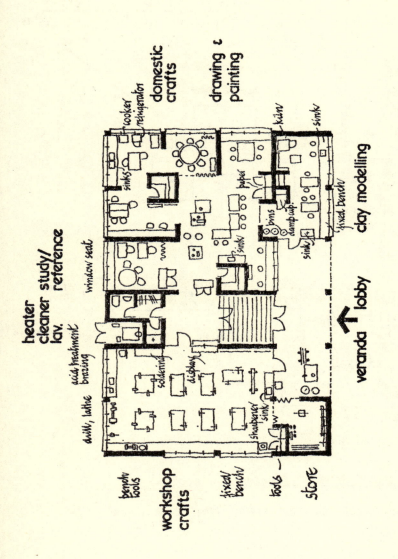

heater
cleaner study/
lav. reference

acid treatment
brazing

window seat

domestic
crafts

drawing &
painting

cooker
refrigerator

sinks

kiln

sink

paper

damp cup

bins

sink

sinks

fixed bench

clay modelling

drill, lathe

veranda   lobby

bench
tools

workshop
crafts

fixed
bench

tools

store

display

soldering

shawbase/
sink

sink

CHAPTER 11

Teachers and Supporting Staff

There will undoubtedly be new and innovatory demands on the teachers. It is a simple matter to change the designation of a school but not so easy to change its teachers . . . . . Teachers who found it relatively easy to measure their success by the traditional methods of formal teaching will find reassurance harder to achieve with the new, less formal approaches suggested for the middle years.

> Tom Gannon and Alan Whalley,
> *(Middle Schools, 1976)*

If you find it difficult to meet with such a tutor as we desire, you are not to wonder. I can only say: Spare no care nor cost to get such an one.

> John Locke,
> *(Some thoughts concerning Education, 1670)*

John Locke was of course right. His concern was to advise on the qualities required of a personal tutor to a young gentleman of good family: but the thoughts he advances in his treatise are of much wider application and will be found remarkably fresh and relevant to the teaching situation to-day. We can no longer afford the luxury of a one-to-one staffing ratio, though the present success of this ratio in the volunteer approach to adult illiteracy through the national campaign 'On the Move' is a reminder of its efficacy where serious educational blockages in an individual have to be overcome; and many teachers do organise periods of individual attention for pupils in special need. But as middle schools develop and the new and innovatory demands on teachers mount, Locke's warning is as valid to the education service to-day as to the noblemen whom he was advising: to achieve the full potential of these new schools, neither care nor cost must be spared to recruit and train good teachers. This is in no way to call for wasteful expenditure; it is rather to get the best possible value from teachers. In an innovatory situation in particular, teachers need training, understanding and support as well as the character, effort and patience which they must bring to their task.

The Task of the Teacher

The teaching force is the most expensive component of the education system, and rightly so; for however good the support and resources at his disposal, it is on the day by day, continuing contact which the teacher has with the pupils that their progress and maturation depends; it is his personality, values, character and skill which set their standards and educate their young minds. His task calls for an indefinable power to communicate, for sensitivity to what is happening in his charges' minds, and for careful and up-to-date selection of the knowledge which he tries to impart. The task is demanding; some teachers are naturally better at it than others, and some make more effort than others. In a profession half a million strong not all can be brilliant, dedicated, innovatory teachers; but two things are clear. One is that the nature and effectiveness of training, both for students and for serving teachers, is crucial to their subsequent performance; the other is that the quality of leadership within a school is vital. Some of the portraits of schools in Chapter 6 give more than an inkling of what that means. In the English education system we give our head teachers great power. Part of the significance of the middle school experience so far is that many of the well led, well equipped and well staffed schools have had unmatched opportunities to innovate and have produced outstanding results in many directions—curricular, social, pastoral. This is an excellent portent, but it is largely through information and training that the achievement of the pacemaker staffs has to be brought within the grasp of their colleagues elsewhere.

The Task of the Head

More than from anything else, a school derives its tone, its atmosphere, its sense of purpose, its enthusiasm for work, its powers of initiative, from the head teacher. There is no blueprint for a successful head in any school except to say that he needs powers of observation and analysis, communication, tolerance and firmness; that he must be educationally well informed and that he needs a measure of experience. In the new medium of the middle school the best heads are those able to inspire experiment and to initiate in the fields of curriculum, organisation and staffing structures; they need to discern what is going well and what is not; and they need a vision of the ideal school which in some degree and in different ways has to influence both staff and pupils. Clarity of thought and expression is essential if others are to understand their aims. Some of these qualities a man or woman is born with; some they learn; and some they can acquire through training. It is significant that in recent years there has been great demand for short courses in the organisation and management of large schools.

Middle schools have the opportunity to innovate as no other type of school at present has. The authoritarian head issuing pronouncements and directives is not likely in this situation to lead educational advance. All the middle schools which are breaking new ground successfully (or at least, all those known to the author) are led by heads who proceed by consultation, discussion and the achievement of a substantial measure of staff unity. The process is seen most clearly in the new schools where head and senior staff were appointed in advance of the school's opening and so had time (even though they may have been still in their previous posts) to consider and define their aims and objectives, to work out patterns of organisation and curriculum, and to set enough down on paper to guide the staff as they took up their appointments. Staff in their turn were brought into the processes of discussion and consultation; and the initial organisation was viewed as provisional and subject to modification in the light of experience. Policies, practices and procedures evolved in this way reflect discussion and a measure of agreement by the whole staff and, even if individual members have reservations about them, they rarely withhold active co-operation. It is a longer process than government by decree from the head's study, but it is a much better basis for an educational community.

The Deployment and Responsibilities of Staff

This assumes an importance unknown in the days of class-teacher based primary schools. It is first a matter of the right teacher with the right assignments in the right place—but not just that, for he has a team responsibility as well, and this calls for a staff structure with clear, but interlocking individual responsibilities. It is easiest to see this in the large 9 to 13 middle school. From the diversity of organisational patterns in use, four principal teacher responsibilities emerge. They interlock in a number of ways, and most teachers are likely to undertake more than one. These responsibilities are:

(1) As *class teacher, class tutor, or group tutor* (there is no uniformity about names). This responsibility is both a pastoral and a teaching one. The tutor is the first point of reference for the pupil; he exercises most of the functions which the class teacher would formerly have undertaken; and is responsible for his overall progress. In the early years the class tutor probably teaches his group for half or more of the week, this amount gradually diminishing as children move up the school and require more specialist tuition.

(2) As *year leader* (again names vary). He leads the teaching team in his year, plans with them the long-term and

short-term development of teaching programmes, organises tutorial and other groups, and maintains continuous assessment and evaluation. His team is composed of both class tutors and specialist teachers, and it is he who is responsible for the correlation and co-ordination of the whole of the work in the year, including thematic or integrated projects in which several teachers join.

(3) As *subject specialist* or *consultant teacher*. He is responsible for a subject and for specific programmes, either alone or in conjunction with teachers in related subjects, throughout the school. Where specialist teaching rooms, facilities and resources are involved, he is responsible for their maintenance, use and oversight. He acts as a consultant to other teachers who participate in the teaching programmes in the subject but who do not themselves have special knowledge of it.

(4) As *leader, head* or *co-ordinator* of a broad curricular area, such as the humanities, languages, social or environmental studies. His is a co-ordinating and integrating rôle, part of his concern being to see that over a period a balance is preserved within the area and that the enthusiasm of individual teachers for a particular subject or aspect does not swamp the others.

There may be other teachers who fill none of these rôles specifically (probationer teachers or part-time teachers among them) but whose whole time is spent teaching without specific pastoral responsibility for a particular group of children. They are usually members of a year team or a subject team or both and take part in appropriate consultations.

There may also be other posts of special responsibility in addition to year leader, subject specialist, or co-ordinator. There is normally a deputy head whose responsibilities, apart from the executive duties implied in the title, will be worked out by the head and himself together; and in a mixed school, if both the head and his deputy are men, there may be a senior mistress who takes care of the welfare of the girls. The number of such posts, and their value in salary terms, depends on a combination of the size of the school and how the head wishes them to be disposed.

Though the pattern of interlocking horizontal (year group) and vertical (subject) teams has commended itself to many of the larger middle schools, it is not universal; but some kind of devolved responsibility and of involvement of as many teachers as possible in the decision-making process is usual. One advantage of the kind of interlocking structure described is that the head has an 'inner cabinet' in the form of year leaders and curricular co-ordinators with whom he can be in constant dialogue. In schools which use the year group team approach regular meetings of at any rate the main members of these teams are also common, and the head keeps in close touch with them too.

In smaller schools the structures can be less formal; and in 8 to 12 schools the full subject specialist is less common than in the 9 to 13 range. But the idea of teachers exercising a consultant rôle in whatever is their main strength has gained ground fast, and the reason is not difficult to see. In a time of vigorous curriculum development such as the last decade, it is virtually impossible for any single teacher to keep abreast of either new knowledge or new teaching approaches in every subject of the curriculum. The volume of reading on the teaching of English and on the nature of language alone could provide full-time occupation for quite a long period, and in the natural, environmental and social sciences too there is a great amount of new material. Even with the help of educational journals, of Schools Council and other publications, and of short in-service training or refresher courses, a teacher cannot remain fully informed in more than a limited field. Moreover, with the success of enquiry methods in stimulating the curiosity of pupils, with curricula which deliberately encourage a wide area of interests, and with the exacting demands of able children to reckon with up to the age of 12 or 13, teachers need the help of better informed colleagues. The institution of the *consultant teacher* not only spreads these responsibilities but involves a large number of members of the staff in a satisfying professional capacity.

Among important special tasks are helping slow learners and retarded pupils on the one hand, and the very able on the other. The former responsibility is widely recognised and all middle schools try to recruit at least one teacher with special knowledge of the field. Methods vary; but whether the children are taught wholly in special groups or withdrawn for part of the time only from their normal age-groups, expert diagnosis, teaching and advice is necessary. A few schools use their remedial education specialist principally to diagnose difficulties and advise how to overcome them without withdrawing children from their normal class, and this pattern of partnership between specialist and class tutor may well spread.

Very able children present different problems. Methods of individual assignment and enquiry, and those which encourage the pupils generally to make use full of the school's resources, are of great value in challenging and satisfying able children; but in their last year or two the degree of stimulus and additional material they need can be very great indeed. Resources, both human and material, may have to be sought outside the school as well as inside. They may include both specially designed curriculum enrichment units such as those under production by the Schools Council, and people and interests in the locality which can be well used by able children. It certainly helps for a member of staff to undertake the responsibility of keeping in touch with such sources and with organisations such as the National Association for Gifted Children; and once again the responsible teacher can do some of his best work by advising his colleagues.

The Composition of Staffs

Many heads have said that, in a 9 to 13 school, their ideal staff would be drawn in equal proportions from three sources: primary schools, secondary schools, and initial training institutions—the first two to provide solid experience of the appropriate age groups of pupils, and the third to introduce the latest ideas and practices and the energy and enthusiasm of youth. A balance of age, sex, temperament, teaching interests and qualifications may also figure, even if unattainably, in the dreams of most heads.

In the early days of middle schools it was the enthusiasts who welcomed the new opportunities, who competed for appointment in the purpose-built schools especially, and who formed highly talented staffs. Where re-organisation of existing schools involved entire staffs already in post, the situation was different, and compromises had to be accepted. Where, as in many country areas, the former village junior school became a middle school simply by keeping its pupils a year longer, receiving their successors a year later, and gaining some additional facilities, the sitting junior school teachers naturally had prior claim and rarely wished to leave. In some boroughs on the other hand the entire teaching force was involved in a total re-organisation on the same day. Such an upheaval, though logical, meant months of meticulous prior planning by the authority and the teachers' representatives, designating each school in its future rôle, woiking out its staffing establishment, and making appointments to the various posts, beginning with the headships and working down. In the city of Hull, for instance, this exercise was carried out painstakingly and with notable success; every teacher had been asked to express his or her preference not only for type of school but also for the actual school of his choice, and a major placing operation in fact met the wishes of more than 90% of the teachers in the borough. Inevitably, sometimes a teacher's preference was given priority over the balance of staffing needs in the school; but on grounds of fair treatment and of maintaining morale the policy was undoubtedly right.

Staffing Ratios

It is difficult to generalise about staffing ratios. The typical schools from which material was drawn to make up the composite examples in Chapter 6 had pupil-teacher ratios of between 19 to 1 and 22 to 1. These are certainly more generous than in 1970, when even in the best placed 9 to 13 schools a figure of 23 to 1 was on the generous side and 25 to 1 not uncommon. Some schools acutely felt the strain in those days, especially when they were giving a great deal of time and effort to building up relations with parents and the outside community, and informed observers certainly felt that such figures were not generous enough. Since 1970, of course, the overall staffing picture in the country has substantially improved, and it is to be hoped that even in difficult economic circumstances it will be held at figures somewhat like those quoted above. There cannot be uniformity, and some authorities have as a matter of policy tried to be especially generous in the early years of a new school's life. Most authorities work to basic ratios for all schools of the same type and size; but the discretion which many show in order to aid schools with special problems, or occasionally in a situation of unusual promise, is often very helpful. The school, after all, does need consideration in the light of its individual circumstances.

Staffing ratios do not of course tell the whole story. Premises influence the flexibility with which staff can be deployed. The range and quality of equipment may affect the degree to which pupils can work on their own. The composition and effectiveness of the supporting staff can make a considerable difference. All in all, however, it is encouraging to record the obvious efforts which authorities have made in recent years to give schools the teachers necessary to extract the fullest advantage from the middle school opportunity.

Qualifications and Training of Teachers

The first generation of middle schools has been staffed by a mixture of teachers whose qualifications and/or experience made them right for the work and of others who just happened to be on the spot when the schools were set up. There were of course no training courses designed to prepare students specifically for work in middle schools until the first few were set up, and even now there are not very many of these. There were three main routes by which, until then, teachers arrived in schools; the position is changing in many ways, particularly now that the aim of an all-graduate profession has been officially accepted, though it will take a long time to achieve.

The first route, a diminishing one, was that of taking a university degree and entering teaching without any course of professional training. It was mainly grammar schools which recruited this kind of specialist graduate, and the route is now closed except for those who gained their degree before 1972. It is unlikely that there are many of these teachers in middle schools. The second route was that of a university degree (or recognised equivalent in other major higher education establishments such as the national colleges and academies of art and music) followed by a year of post-graduate professional training in a university department of education; for some years now colleges of education have also offered these one-year professional courses for graduates. The third was through a college of education which prepared students solely for teaching; before 1962 a two-year course led to the status of qualified teacher, but since then the course has lasted three years—or four for academically able students who wished in addition to secure the Bachelor of Education (B.Ed.) degree. Traditionally, the second route produced graduates with specialist qualifications in one subject or a small group of subjects, and most of them entered secondary schools. The third route, via the colleges of education, was responsible for providing almost all the primary teachers; but many colleges also ran a *junior/secondary* course based upon the studies of 7 to 13 or 14 year old children, and students from these courses entered primary and secondary schools in about equal numbers. The *junior/secondary* courses were not however middle school courses; they studied children in the middle years, and curricular matters for the same age-range, but they did not examine middle school potentialities, structures and problems. Since 1968, however, when the first

Science on the doorstep; weather recording group at work.

Science in the lab; the end-product of an embryology study.

middle school course was set up in a college, a number of others have followed, and have proved popular with a considerable number of students who wish to teach in middle schools.

The whole structure of teacher training in England and Wales is now undergoing radical change, which there is no space to describe here; but significant consequences are likely to be the move towards graduate status for all new teachers and the increasing proportion of new teachers holding specialist qualifications. Some educationists fear that the good general teacher, for so long so valuable in primary schools, may be sharply reduced in numbers; if this should happen it would undoubtedly change the character not only of primary schools but of 8 to 12 middle schools, and perhaps of many of the 9 to 13 middle schools also.

Middle school staffs have been filled by teachers from both the second and third routes, and many have at their disposal an excellent range of talent, qualification and experience. Exact figures are hard to come by, but the widespread impression is that 9 to 13 schools generally have from one half to two thirds graduates on their staffs—though a curious pointer from a recent DES survey is that a high proportion of the graduates may actually not be teaching the subjects in which they specialised in their university degree. One can only speculate on the reasons, but it is clearly unsafe to correlate the performance of a staff with its initial qualifications; experience is at least as strong a determinant. What may need careful scrutiny is whether there are any subjects or aspects of the curriculum in which middle school performance is low, and if so, how far this relates to gaps in initial training. Immediate remedies would, of course, have to be sought mainly through in-service training, which in any case has a major part to play.

In-service Training

Training for the first middle school staffs was naturally bound to be in-service training; and so far it has served the middle school field well.

It has two marked advantages. The first is that much of it is truly locally based and therefore available to a larger number of serving teachers than residential courses or long-term courses away from home. Programmes can be adapted to the most convenient local attendance patterns, evenings, full days, or week-ends. The second is that, since the clientele consists of serving teachers in the locality, they know what is likely to be of most service to them and the programmes can be designed to meet their needs. The situation is not static; needs change, and training provision should adapt to meet new ones.

There will naturally be some courses which cannot be provided locally, for instance in subjects of the curriculum for which there may not be enough demand—in French, for instance, or rural science which may not be provided in all schools. But experience has shown that courses in English language, mathematics, science and religious education are invariably well attended, as also are those on topics such as record-keeping, assessment, school, class and group organisation. A further valuable facility which teachers' centres may offer is demonstrations and explanations of new apparatus and classroom kits, project material and of course books. A welcome allied feature has been the part which some middle schools have been playing in trials of various Schools Council project kits; and there is no reason why this should be confined to national projects. There are examples of local teachers' study groups devising their own materials and courses for experimental use, the members of the groups then trying them out in their own schools and returning to evaluate and proceed further.

In the earliest years of preparation, areas like the West Riding, Hull, Merton, Southampton and others found that courses and study groups on the general issues such as organisation, management, syllabus construction, assessment of pupils' progress, and the use of buildings were of great value. In the second stage refresher courses to improve competence in actual subjects and techniques emerged as the major demand. The most recent development in well established middle school areas is demand, not so much for guidance in middle school applications of curricular material or theories, but simply for news of new thinking and of innovation generally. Interest in major educational issues is keen, but teachers no longer press to be told what the precise applications in middle schools are. This development is encouraging, for it means that there is a growing measure of confidence in their ability to work out these applications for themselves.

One regrettable facet of the present scene is the lack of national conferences and forums at which middle school experience can be shared and problems or lines of development pursued in common. Reference has been made to one such conference at the University of Bradford in 1975 which made an excellent start at identifying common problems, set up a number of curriculum study groups to work throughout the winter, and should have been followed by a second conference to evaluate their work. Unfortunately the worsening financial situation resulted in the withdrawal of much support and the follow-up conference had to be cancelled. This constitutes a lost opportunity at a time when the first generation of middle schools has been running long enough to feel established in its policies and principles, and when the second and third generations are eager for help and formative debate; it is to be hoped that the setback will be brief.

Supporting Staff

No general picture can be given of supporting staff or even, in precise terms, of the need for them. Needs vary with the size and nature of the school; the practices of authorities differ quite widely; and individual schools may have their own preferences about the exact kind of support. Probably all that can usefully be said is that the more energy and time teachers can conserve for the main professional task of teaching and of planning and preparing for it, the better; and that there are three kinds of direct support for them—secretarial, technical and welfare.

The scale of secretarial assistance in schools is decided locally. There should be no encouragement to anyone, head or staff, to multiply paper unnecessarily; but correspondence has to be answered, returns have to be made, information has to be conveyed to parents and outside bodies, while within the school syllabuses, lesson material, excursion sheets, notes and records all generate work of a clerical, not of a teaching, nature. In some schools a dictating machine available for use by at least senior members of staff has been found a considerable time-saver. The area is one for careful enquiry and reasoned decision.

Technical assistance concerns principally valuable teaching equipment, audio-visual aids, workshop machines, and scientific apparatus. When these are lying idle expensive plant is out of use and teaching programmes may be restricted. How maintenance and repair is best undertaken, whether by a technician based in the school (who can often then give useful help in setting up apparatus and in handling projectors and similar machines during lessons), or one serving a group of schools, or by some other method, is a local matter; but systems involving a reporting procedure through a distant office and a wait for an outside contractor all too frequently seem to result in long delays and staff exasperation.

Assistance involves other services, but no school can cut itself off from giving practical help as well as passing information. A few middle schools now have a health and welfare assistant who can relieve other staff of a good deal of detailed work and, in conjunction with the regular visits of school doctor and nurse, can build up a picture of the health and well-being of individual children and prove of service to both school and parents.

These are not of course the only members of staff in addition to the teachers, but there is no need to survey the complete range of supporting services. What is significant is the way in which, in common with schools of other types in recent years, the best middle schools regard their ancillary staffs as full members of the school community and treat them as such; in a few schools they rank as members of the staff common room, and in many they share in school and social occasions along with the teaching staff. This is not only a means of commanding loyalty; it is social education in practice, to be seen by parents and children.

CHAPTER 12

Beyond the Gates

The school is concerned with two contact areas beyond its gates—with other schools, and with family, home and community. The idea that teachers should give time and energy, in addition to their full-time teaching commitments, to contacts of this sort is relatively new; thirty years ago such contacts were slight, and even to-day their extent varies very much from school to school. To-day, however, few teachers would dispute the need; the justification is simply that a child's educational progress is undoubtedly affected, for good or ill, by his experiences outside the school and that if the school itself can influence some of them for his good, then it should.

1.   Links with Other Schools

We have seen that it is widely accepted that children's learning is a continuous, evolving process which ought not to be subjected to sudden shocks or interruptions. As the middle link of the chain of experience, the middle school is particularly involved. If it is to respect and reinforce this continuity, it must know where it stands in the total process, what learning experiences the pupils have had in their preceding school, and what awaits them when they move out of the middle school into the next stage. And this is not merely a matter of broad general ideas (though they are better than no knowledge at all) but of the actual experiences of the individual pupil. Good working contact with first and upper schools is therefore a necessity—knowing their aims and objectives, the range and organisation of their curricula, their general characteristics and atmosphere, and their view of individual children.

190

In the middle school areas the organisational structure is generally either pyramidal or linear. The pyramid structure is logical; a number of first schools, which have the advantage of being small and local, feed into a larger middle school, and in their turn a number of middle schools feed into a larger upper school. The number and location of the schools forming the pyramid depends on the spread of population in the area, on ease of access, transport, and availability of school sites. This structure was easier to achieve in areas of expanding population or where for other reasons some new school building was possible. The linear structure consists simply of one first school feeding one middle school, either on the same site or close by; and it is inherited from the common pattern of one infants school feeding one junior school. It is found in areas where, because the population was static or declining and new school building could not be justified, the natural step was simply to change the use of the two former schools. The extreme form of linear structure is the 5 to 12 *combined school*.

(i)   LINKS WITH FIRST SCHOOLS

In linear structure areas there are—or should be—few difficulties in the way of liaison between the middle school and its contributory first school, since a short walk across the playground can bring individual teachers or entire staffs together. The actual extent of communication depends in the main on the temperament of the two head teachers; where they wish it to happen, contact is close. Frequent informal conversation between them and, especially in the summer term before the September transfers, exchanges of visits between the teachers of the top classes in the first school and those of the first-year classes in the middle school, are now found virtually everywhere, and often contacts extend well beyond this. The first school children may be allowed the use of some of the middle school facilities (hall, music or visual aids room), not only to widen their own activities but also to familiarise them with the middle school before they become members of it. Middle school teachers may do some work with the older children in the first school, and sometimes first school teachers who like contact with older children have similar opportunities in the middle school; in any case the teachers often informally exchange visits. Frequently the middle school invites the first school children to be its guests at special productions—concerts, plays, Christmas carols, and so on. The opportunities for forging links in both the children's learning and their social experience can be particularly good when schools are so close, and often the middle school teachers of the first year will have a good personal knowledge of the individual children before the September transfer, so that any meetings or forwarding of records then fills out details already partly familiar.

Under the pyramid structure, where as many as half a dozen first schools may feed into a middle school, more organised measures to create and maintain links are necessary. The same exchange of visits by teachers may—probably will—take place; but, unless the middle school is well enough staffed to designate a single teacher to undertake the assignment of visiting all the contributory schools, the visits will be more infrequent and spread over more of the middle school staff. Personal knowledge of individual children is more difficult to gain, and the nature and quality of written records therefore becomes more important, though this is not to say that the records themselves need to be more detailed. All education authorities supply official record cards for completion and transfer, but many teachers would say that the most important work on record to transmit is a folder of the child's recent work in all the main branches (writing, painting, mathematics, science) with a list of the books he has recently read and with teachers' comments on his progress, preferences and problems, if any. His personal characteristics and the manner of his approaches to learning may be of greater interest to the middle school teachers than his actual attainment in measurable skills, though these will also be welcome.

One other feature which the good middle school usually wishes to know is the general approach to teaching and learning used in the individual first schools. Many are open and informal in their approach; others may be more strictly organised with, perhaps, some prescribed time-tables and with defined levels of attainment in the basic skills which it is hoped all children will reach; naturally many go well beyond. Some first schools place their children in *vertical* or *family groups* in which pupils of two or three age groups (5 to 8, for instance, or 7 to 9) are taught together; others rely on the traditional grouping of one age-group to a class. Some enjoy new buildings of open-plan design in which for a good part of the day children can be given freedom to move around freely, while others are still in old buildings in which such free movement is hardly practicable and where more controlled patterns of working are necessary. Since it may draw on schools working in such differing situations and ways, the middle school clearly needs to know them.

Formal meetings of the head of a middle school with the heads of his contributory schools as a body seem to be rare. Exchanges of visits, usually informal, are common, and among colleagues who know each other well the ground can be covered without a specific agenda; written records later supplement the personal exchanges. Visits are not indeed confined to heads; class teachers too, or members of the team teaching in the entry year of the middle school, often join in these exchanges. Many of the actual details of the teaching are useful to the middle school staffs, such as the way in which their contributory schools tackle reading, writing, number, and mathematical experience. Where a group of first school heads talk these matters over with their middle school colleague, practices in both schools can be more closely aligned; and what is true of the basic skills may be true too of many other areas of learning.

Since the achievement of schools must reflect the strengths and interests of their staffs, some do especially well in art, others in music, others in movement, others in appreciation of the living world, and so on. Few middle school heads would wish to exchange this diversity for uniformity; but it certainly helps to know what to expect and to be able to plan to build on it. Formal meetings are far from being the only way of ensuring this; many prefer a regular exchange by different teachers throughout the year, or 'open days' in each school when colleagues from the others come to observe, talk and listen. What does matter is that there shall be definite channels for the exchange and passage of information, and that staffs as well as heads shall know what they are and use them.

(ii)　LINKS WITH UPPER SCHOOLS

Pressure on middle schools from upper schools has at some times and in some places been strong; again, both have much to gain from effective and well-founded links. In the early days these sometimes took the form of upper schools in effect trying to prescribe what middle schools should cover in various fields of the curriculum, and it must be said at once that links should denote partnership, and that neither partner has the right to impose requirements on the other. Let the links be effective, by all means, and particularly in the curricular field, since this is the biggest worry of the upper school; but true effectiveness is achieved only by sustained joint work on the topics which worry either partner, and this must be prepared by a readiness to hear and understand the point of view of the other.

That said, the anxieties of the upper school are not difficult to understand. The memory of the traditional entry to secondary schools at the age of 11 is still strong, and secondary school staffs then naturally thought in terms of a four year course from entry to the minimum school leaving age of 15 and a five year course to the first public examinations, G.C.E. 'O' Level and C.S.E. In a three or four tier organisation which includes middle schools, the upper schools now receive pupils not at 11 but at 12 or 13, and for former secondary teachers it has been difficult not to think in terms of 'losing a year'—or two years. Despite their later entry to the upper schools, pupils have still to be presented for the public examinations at the age of 16, and in some schools as many as 60 per cent of all the pupils stay for this. Formerly, the secondary schools were able to regard their first two years as diagnostic, to assess the abilities and the aptitudes of pupils without pressure and so to ensure that their pupils made securely based curricular choices from the age of 13 on. Many upper schools are unhappy about the later entry; either they must delay the start of some of their examination courses and then have to hurry them, or they must accept the advice of their contributory middle schools. If the latter are not well acquainted with the upper schools' internal situation, that advice may be wrong. Clearly there is need for close and continuing consultation, and even so the problem is a teasing one and no clear formulae have emerged capable of general application.

A two-fold responsibility lies on the middle schools. In the first place they should prepare their pupils, in knowledge and in attitudes, for life in the school to which they next go. So far as down-to-earth detail is concerned, this is not too difficult, given goodwill between the two schools and a little organisation; explanations about the upper school, its internal organisation, time-tabling, working conventions and so on, supplemented by one or more familiarisation visits to the school during the term preceding transfer, probably suffice. Very many middle and upper schools do now co-operate to arrange this, and the upper schools show themselves in general to be gracious hosts. But if pupils are in addition to be psychologically prepared and to have the right expectations about life in the upper school, more is required. During the final year in the middle school there must be a gradual change in methods of working, in presentation and assessment of work, and in the nature of the work itself. If this is carefully done, without sudden shocks or changes, the pupils should acclimatise easily to the new organisation because they bring with them the confidence which arises from knowing what may be expected of them—in routines, in more closely time-tabled programmes, in more specialist teaching, indeed in all those aspects of school life the cumulative effect of which can be confusion and educational setback if the change has not been well prepared. The middle school can only discharge this responsibility if it is familiar with the objectives and the practices of the upper school, and if teachers from both have talked the problems over together. How the necessary contacts are made constitutes a local administrative exercise in which, because it is the focus of a number of middle schools, probably the upper school should take the lead; the essential is that it should be done in a spirit of partnership, of which there are many successful examples.

Its second responsibility is more strictly curricular. Probably most upper schools have come to terms with the fact that in many middle schools much of the work is geared to the individual or the small group, and that the pupils in a year-group may not all have covered the same ground. (The idea is not, of course, unknown to upper schools, many of which themselves employ such approaches for some purposes and in some subjects.) Provided that the pupils have learned to acquire and to apply knowledge, the best upper schools are no longer disconcerted by this individual variety, especially when it is accompanied by keen interest, by ability to concentrate and to work alone as well as in a group, and by a ready adaptability to new methods. But this will not happen unless the middle schools as a group are willing to work with their upper school. The problem is best illustrated by examples, and two apposite ones are foreign languages and mathematics.

The first foreign language in this country is traditionally French, and all first and second year upper school pupils are likely to learn it. But what is their starting point to be? If there are six contributory middle schools and there has been no co-ordination, there may well be two which have already given their pupils a four-year course, one a two-year course, one through exigencies of staff an erratic now-we-have-it-now-we-don't provision, one no French at all, and one originally minded school which instead has provided German. What is the languages department of the upper school to do? One can hardly blame its members if they decide to ignore the preceding chaos and start everyone at the beginning—which is quite unfair to the pupils, some of whom will be happily whisked along, some bored at covering again ground they have covered already, some rebellious at losing their German, and some confused because their group is so heterogeneous that orderly teaching rapidly becomes impossible. Nor does the confusion necessarily stop there. Teachers of modern languages are to-day generally agreed upon the need for oral work as the basis of the early stages of learning, and the audio-visual courses developed in recent years and widely used in primary and middle schools assume this; but the question that worries many specialist modern language departments in upper schools is how far the qualifications and competence of teachers of French in the lower schools can be trusted. It is notoriously difficult, for instance, to correct an inaccurate accent or intonation once pupils have acquired it; and DES statements confirm that there is still a shortage of adequately qualified language teachers. Clearly language policy ought to be thrashed out by all the schools in the group.

A second example can be furnished from the field of mathematics. Broadly speaking, until 20 years ago there had been little change in mathematics teaching for a century or more. The foundation in the early years was basic arithmetic and computation, accompanied by memorisation and continual practice of such basic processes and devices as the four rules and number bonds. In all that time teaching methods and material had remained virtually unchanged. Algebra, geometry and trigonometry were regarded as more advanced studies to be approached, other than with the most able children, only in the secondary course; to-day, the assumption that they are necessarily more difficult has been generally discarded. Changes came in the 1950s. The ground was cleared by new theories of learning, and particularly by those propounded by the Swiss researcher, Jean Piaget. Practising mathematicians such as Lancelot Hogben and Geoffrey Matthews applied these theories in practical ways to the teaching of mathematics, and so there came into being what has become loosely known as *the new mathematics,* a somewhat unsatisfactory term since the only thing that is new about many of the concepts is their introduction into the school curriculum. One of the principal features is that young children are introduced to, and helped by practical experience to understand, mathematical concepts such as space, size, volume, shape, distance, and to appreciate relationships between articles of different size, volume, shape and so on, before they are required to learn the basic tools of calculation such as the multiplication tables and the four rules. They thus see purpose in the business of calculation when they come to it and are not dulled by meaningless memorisation.

New apparatus, new objectives and new material have all sprung from these new approaches, and to those brought up on the older traditional methods the new look may well appear utterly different. As with any reform, the pace of acceptance is uneven, and, though in many areas in-service training has been eagerly taken up by the teachers, there is no guarantee that all the contributory middle schools in a group will be working along similar lines. Moreover, mathematics in upper schools has felt the wind of change, and there is no uniformity at this level either. If pupils are not to be plunged into confusion on transfer, there must be consultation by all the schools of a group, and, one would hope, a measure of agreement about content, method and sequence.

These two examples demonstrate that the days are past when any single school should insist on self-contained independence in curricular matters. The internal freedom of the individual school to do this has long been cherished in English education; wherever the statutory responsibility may lie (and this appears to be divided between the local education authority and the governors of a school), in practice the head and his staff have planned the curriculum for their school. But in the interests of the pupils, it is now vital that at important points of transfer there should not be confusing changes of direction, content or method, and decisions need to be taken by the staffs of upper school and contributory middle schools working in concert; if this means the sacrifice of a measure of individual freedom, it is nevertheless for the good of the pupils who must pass through both stages and for whose welfare the schools exist.

It is vital that consultation shall be genuine; there must be no attempt to impose. Decisions must be taken as a real exercise in partnership by representatives of all the schools concerned, and they must reflect what middle schools can reasonably undertake in the light of their staffing and resources; they are not there simply to follow blueprints of what the upper school would like. The upper school likewise must be prepared to give up some of its own freedom. Its first year syllabuses must clearly be designed with regard to agreed policies and to the probable attainments and working habits of the pupils entering from the middle schools. Nor should upper school syllabuses be substantially changed without consultation with the middle school staffs.

There is no need for individual initiative to be stifled. Agreement can often be a matter of general principle rather than of detail, though in subjects such as languages where the techniques and sequence are particularly important it may be wise to include them. In wide-ranging fields such as science it may be sufficient to agree on a range of basic topics which it is desirable that all the middle schools should include as part of their courses. Probably the most important start to any curricular consultations is to define the objectives, and in many fields this will still leave a great deal open. In history, for instance, where the creation of interest and a feeling for the past is likely to be a major objective, study of virtually any period or culture can contribute and the middle schools need by no means be restricted to specific periods or specific topics through the ages. The definition of objectives for the teaching of art, music, literature and local studies would no doubt leave a similar breadth of choice open to the individual school; what is important is that the upper school is aware before the September transfers of what has actually been going on.

The mechanism and frequency of consultations between upper and contributory middle schools should naturally be adapted to local circumstances. Full scale conferences, other than as a preliminary to area reorganisations, have been found of only limited use. Detailed discussions on the various curricular areas are, experience shows, best carried out by small working groups which report to and discuss further with the staffs of all the schools as they proceed. These need not—indeed, should not—be confined to subjects or to precise areas of knowledge; such topics as integrated approaches and multi-disciplinary projects are important to many middle schools and deserve study in such groups.

One very real difficulty is finding time for these exercises, especially since the staffing ratios of many middle schools make the release of more than one or two members of staff at a time, even for short periods, difficult. In one or two instances they have given up a day of their half-term break or of one of their main holidays for the purpose. In others a so-called *occasional holiday* has been taken by all the schools; pupils have had the day off while the staffs have all come in to work. But these arrangements suffer from the disadvantage that, from the middle schools' side especially, some teachers will be needed on more than one working party. Whatever form the mechanism takes, it is to be hoped that the local education authority will continue to regard these meetings as educational engagements of high importance; the record of many is excellent, and special acknowledgement is due to the work of LEA advisers.

Where middle schools have been in operation for some time the question arises of how often such meetings need to continue. It is the local participants who must judge; but it would seem that some contact at the working party level ought to be maintained each year, even if it takes the form of interchange of visits rather than of actual meetings. While

The present yields strange things too; a farm study.

Art display — explaining to visitors.

The M.P. calls; young constituents add to their knowledge of government.

nothing is more dull than unnecessary meetings, it is easy to drift imperceptibly into a state of believing that full contact is being maintained when in fact the situation inside the schools has changed or is changing. There is perhaps virtue in a thorough evaluation every few years, whether conducted by the staffs themselves or by an outside group.

It would be wrong to pretend that this level or degree of consultation yet exists in all middle school areas; but it should. Fortunately the trend is markedly in that direction. A survey conducted in 1975 by the Assistant Masters' Association, which has members in both upper and middle schools, and which concluded with a one-day conference, led to the publication of a very useful report in the following year. The difficulties and problems were frankly recorded, the achievements and shortcomings of middle schools were appraised, and the state of curricular co-operation and co-ordination was closely scrutinised. The general tone was encouraging, and areas where co-operation was as yet imperfect nevertheless accepted the need for it. One advance which the conference thought practicable concerned records; it was suggested that if upper schools made greater use of the records compiled and forwarded to them by middle schools, and if they adopted a common core curriculum in their first year based not upon single subjects but upon fields of study, as so many middle schools do, courses could more easily be matched to the needs of the pupils and the first year need no longer be used as a diagnostic year.

In the early years of middle schools many upper school teachers regarded them with marked reserve, fearing that educational standards would suffer. That this fear is now overcome is evident from the concluding paragraph of the report, *The Middle School System*.

The consensus of opinion among these members is that the middle school system is a viable one, that it can be a most satisfactory way of organising the education of children in the age-range 8 to 13, that the education of the children in the particular age-range 11 to 13 can be as complete and successful as in other systems of organisation *if* there is an adequate supply of teachers of the appropriate calibre, the material resources are available, the conditions of service are satisfactory and, above all, there is a willingness on the part of all the teachers (and the opportunities to do so) to co-operate with their colleagues in the other part of the system.

As the final clause implies, co-operation is a two-way partnership involving all the teachers in both middle and upper schools. It may in the long run prove the most significant link of all.

2. *Links with Home and Family*

How far should the task of the teacher extend? There is no single or simple answer. In some European countries the tradition is that the teacher is the expert in purveying knowledge, that his business is to do this with all his energies and all his skill, and that his responsibilities end there; what his pupils do, and how they are cared for, outside the school is for others, and primarily for parents. Such an exclusive view has never commanded whole-hearted support in England, though there are teachers who hold it; and fifty years ago, with classes of fifty or more in elementary schools and no free periods, it was only the exceptional teacher who could do much more —but the concern was often there, and in the economic depressions of the 1920s and 1930s many teachers did much for the welfare and the leisure activities of their pupils. Formal links with homes and with organisations in the community may have been few, but of personal links there were many, however unorganised.

In the 1960s it became plain that schools could no longer hold parents or the community at arm's length. The whole of society and the relationships within it were becoming more open—with attendant opportunities, no doubt, but also attendant risks. The growing emancipation of children from parental discipline could bring consequences either good or bad, and certainly had to be reckoned with. The growing indifference of some parents to the progress of their children, the increasing number of working mothers with their 'latchkey children' locked out of the home from the time mother left for work to the time when she returned, the lower marrying ages with consequent increase in the number of young, insecure mothers, were all developments which responsible bodies of teachers could not ignore; and, if the lot of the children was to be improved, this could only effectively be done through contact with their parents. Links were certainly needed.

At the same time the demand for adult education was growing, both to fill periods of leisure and to improve career qualifications. Education was news, and new organisations sprang up which concerned themselves with it directly or indirectly. The face of many communities was changing too— in new towns and in the vast new housing developments around old cities drastically and often unhappily so, for they were often without roots and without resources. It was becoming urgently necessary to interest and involve the adults of to-morrow in the community of to-day, to observe, to understand, and to plan for its improvement. Links were needed here too.

Less than twenty years ago it was a commonplace in some areas to find a notice just inside the school gates in terms like these: *Visitors are not permitted to pass this point unless they have business with the Head Teacher*. And visitors emphatically included parents! Even some senior members of the leading teachers' associations were strongly opposed to parents entering schools for any but formal purposes. To-day, if any such notices survive, they must be but few. Change was of course already on the way twenty years ago, and several factors combined to accelerate it. The first was the growing volume of evidence from psychological and sociological sources, as well as from the pragmatic experience of the teaching profession, that the strongest single influence on the growing child was his home, his family and especially his parents. J. H. B. Douglas summed up much of the evidence in his book *Home and School* in 1964, and three years later close and effective links between school and home were urged as one of the major priorities advocated in the Plowden Report. The logic, in face of the evidence, was clear. If the parents are hostile towards the school or if they are apathetic about what the child does there, they will not give him much encouragement. To gain their understanding and sympathy and to change this kind of attitude is the surest way of improving the performance of their children. How can this be done without real and effective personal links? The short answer is that it cannot. The degree of interest and support shown by the parents is either an unseen accelerator or an unseen brake, and more and more teachers resolved to try to take the brake off.

FORMAL CONTACTS

There are, broadly speaking, two types of contact between home and school, the formal and the informal. All schools have to maintain some formal contact with parents. At its simplest this takes the form of the occasional note of information about dates of terms and holidays, forth-coming functions, invitations to attend a child's medical examination, and some kind of termly report on the child's educational progress. But even the report, which is the most important of these links, can vary from the stereotyped and reticent to the personal and informative. There can be few readers who are not familiar with the former, often a printed pro-forma with a series of headings for each subject or aspect of the curriculum and one or two more for such characteristics as conduct, co-operation, and application to work—the comments under each being usually a brief judgment in a phrase or even a single word, with little or none of the evidence underlying the judgment. But a change has come over reports in many schools—and some middle schools have pioneered in evolving new styles—so that, although the basic information is still briefly given, the rest of the report is much more informative.

One paragraph may tell of the child's scholastic progress, another of his creative, imaginative and artistic talents, a third of his personality as those teachers who know him best see it, and a fourth of his strengths and weaknesses. Finally his class teacher, group tutor or year leader sums up, and the head may conclude with a suggestion or two about the kind of help which the parents might give. The Plowden Report was able to quote examples of this more personal reporting as long ago as 1967, and it is often particularly appropriate to the formative middle school years in which children can mature and change very quickly.

Most schools which restrict contacts to the formal will have some occasions in the year when parents are invited for special reasons—a school play or concert, a meeting to explain to parents of pupils in their final year the arrangements for the forthcoming transfer of their children to an upper school, and probably one or more evenings during the year when parents are invited to inspect their children's work and to ask the teachers about it; discussion has often to be brief in view of the queue of other parents waiting for the same purpose. Few schools nowadays would do less than this. The disadvantage of a programme which does not go beyond this is that it does little positively to attract the uninterested parent or those who are nervous of contacts with authority.

INFORMAL CONTACTS

The informal contacts which many schools practise with much success are based on the principle of the *open door,* that is to say, that parents are welcome at any time. In practice this rarely means that the school is flooded with parents; but it does mean that the father who is worried about his child and who works nights can call during the first hour of the morning and know that some-one (the head, a house tutor, or a year leader) will see him, or that the working mother hurrying home in the last hour of afternoon school can do the same. Some of the new purpose built middle schools include, or have set aside, a room or part of a foyer or similar area for parents to meet and talk among themselves, and for staff to drop in and take part briefly; this indeed is where many ideas are born and problems ironed out. If a parent wishes to see a local study, or some new mathematics, or to hear her son's music group at work, in this kind of school the visitor is welcome for such purposes without formality. There is often a standing invitation on certain days of the week to parents to join in school or year assemblies and to stay on to see something of the work going on afterwards. Easy relationships flow from this kind of practice, and give both sides confidence to talk together.

It is moreover common in these schools to find parents actually at work—not attempting the professional task of the teacher but saving them time by taking off their shoulders some of the time-consuming tasks that have to be done. Library books have to be checked and covered; stocks of consumable materials have to be given out for art and craft lessons; small groups of pupils need some-one to see or hear what they have done; the detail of school visits has to be prepared, and so on. Sometimes a parent who is a craftsman or technician will be able to explain better than the teacher could how a pocket calculator works or how printed circuits for use in transistor radios are produced; or an enthusiast may be able to interpret bird and animal tracks in the spinney or tell a group how to identify certain constellations and stars in the night sky. Many schools are conscious that in the skills and talents of their parents they have a substantial additional reserve of knowledge and expertise, which is often willingly offered for the good of the school.

A feature of the last thirty years has been the growth of parent-teacher associations (generally known as P.T.As) with a constitution, officers (usually elected from among staff and parents), and a committee which draws up programmes in which as a rule social evenings alternate with evenings given to directly educational topics. Though every head teacher is aware that social evenings tend to be better patronised than the others, nevertheless the programmes as a whole can not only cement friendly relations between teachers and parents but also contribute towards parent education. The mix of activities may vary according to the neighbourhood. The period under review has seen in middle class areas particularly the development of keen interest among parents in the education their children are receiving, not infrequently to the point of putting pressure on heads to deliver results in the shape of literate, numerate children able to gain entry to selective secondary or upper schools; the pressure has not entirely disappeared even with the introduction of comprehensive schools, since these parents continue to assess for themselves whether the education their children are receiving is a good foundation for later success in GCE examinations and in the battle for entry to higher education. There has often been much suspicion of the more liberal discovery approaches to the curricular work and of developments like the *new mathematics* or *Nuffield science*. Many heads have found the programmes of the P.T.As a useful channel for securing the understanding of parents. In more largely working class areas, on the other hand, the focus may be different. The Plowden Report quoted an example of a primary school on a new housing estate where no common action or sense of community existed until the head suggested to parents the benefit that could come to school and community from a swimming pool, which they then literally built with their own hands, forming lasting relationships in the process. In that particular case parent and community education was a natural rubbing-off process, and in many places this is effective where formally educative programmes would not be.

Not all schools have P.T.As. In some the heads prefer to work without any formal body, usually on the grounds that some of the parents whom they most need to reach (they think especially of the socially nervous, the apathetic, and the disadvantaged) are the very ones who would hold aloof from anything organised. In others organisations open their membership more widely than to parents alone, using such titles as the Meadowvale School Association or the Friends of Meadowvale School. In a few places the association is a Parents' Association and the staff are invited as guests. There is variety, in fact, reflecting the characteristics of a district, the stage which the thinking on both sides has reached, and, sometimes, the personalities involved.

The measure of change is however indicated by the growth in membership of the National Confederation of Parent-Teacher Associations, which, from a two-figure membership of constituent associations in the mid-1960s, now numbers some 1500 and runs a well established network of information services, publications, and an annual national conference. If the energy of its founder, John Hale, himself a primary school head, is largely responsible, nevertheless such advance could not have taken place had the public mood not been thoroughly in sympathy with it. Another body which names close parent-teacher co-operation as one of its objectives is CASE (the Confederation for the Advancement of State Education) which, like the NCPTA, is a federation of autonomous local branches. The two bodies are the major partners in the Home and School Council, a national body which receives some support from public funds and which has produced some extremely useful inexpensive handbooks on matters of concern to both teachers and parents such as current trends in primary education, the involvement of parents in the curriculum, and the rôle of governors and managers.

The involvement of middle schools with parents is often lively and shows itself in many ways; there has been space to mention only some of these. The age-band of their pupils gives these schools a distinctive opportunity. They are local schools, in most places accessible with reasonable ease to most parents—unlike many schools in the next stage of education which serve extensive areas. The schools themselves are for the most part not too large for easy personal contact between parents and at least some of the staff. Finally, the middle school years are for the children years of such rapid yet often uneven development, and of such changes of personality as they mature and discover themselves, that periodic dialogue between their parents and their teachers can be helpful to both parties and can enhance the support which both give—or should wish to give—to their maturing charges.

3. Links with the Community

The nature and quality of what can be done varies with the area. In a small market town with a long established sense of community the school and its staff, or some of them at least, are usually well known and may be influential in the affairs of the town. In a commuter suburb on the other hand there may be no such identity and the attempt to make neighbourhood links may be discouraging and difficult. In an inner city area with a multi-racial and perhaps polyglot population the need for links with the disparate elements in the local community may be very clear, but actually to set them up can again be a delicate and difficult process. Nevertheless the record of many middle schools is good.

The first essential is that the school should know the local community—its character, its occupations, its institutions, its prejudices, strengths and weaknesses. This is true first of all for the staff; and it is no doubt helpful if they themselves live in the community. Just how difficult this can be is summed up in the words of one inner city head when he said 'The only thing some of my staff know about this locality is the way from the school to the bus stop'—through no fault of their own in that particular case, where local housing policies gave newly arrived teachers little chance of living locally. But it is not only the staff; it is a vital part of the children's education too to come to know and understand what their local community is, how it became like it, and what might be done to develop or improve it. This is in part a curricular matter, and as such receives attention in most middle schools —but it extends beyond the curriculum too. It is the more important that the middle school should do this where the upper school to which children transfer is some distance away, since, although local studies and community involvement may continue there, the community will be a larger and possibly a different one (if, for instance, the change is from village to town.) But in any case there is likely to be more time for local studies in the middle school than in the upper, and children in the middle school years are very receptive to this kind of investigative study.

Next, the community needs to know the school. It is doubtful whether much can be done through formal links, though there are one or two. There has been a strong recent trend by local education authorities to set up for each middle school its own governing or managing body, instead of the omnibus sub-committees which under many authorities used to act for so many schools that they rarely had effective knowledge of any of them. (Governing and managing bodies are local bodies which are responsible for broad over-sight of the school and the quality of the education given in it; subject to the confirmation of the LEA, they appoint the head teacher and may also suspend him and recommend his dismissal. They meet formally once a term but it is hoped that in addition members maintain continuing contact with the school through visits and other means.) The constitution of the governing or managing body is determined by the LEA and is subject to the approval of the DES; the body itself is a statutory one and is meant to provide a channel for local interest in the school and a means of communication with the LEA. The membership includes voluntary members nominated by the LEA, who are rarely professional educationists but should be local citizens interested in education; it often includes also representatives of the teaching staff and of parents, both these categories being elected. Where this is done, there is a real chance of effective communication between school, parents, and community.

The second body which can be involved is the authority itself, in the shape of the elected members and of the professional staff of the education department. Councillors can and should know the schools in their wards, and the schools are of course entitled and wise to invite them from time to time and to make friends of them. Though pressures on administrative staff are often intense, some chief education officers and other senior members of their services do make a point of keeping some time free to visit schools; and the growth in recent years of advisory services provides another link.

Informal links with the community around have usually to be initiated by the school. Curricular local studies put them in touch with some organisations and with some individuals, and continuing contacts may result. Churches, libraries, museums; suitable branches of local services such as the planning and surveying departments, social welfare organisations, both statutory and voluntary; suitable local employers; community and charitable organisations; the local newspapers and, for the fortunate schools, local radio stations; these are examples of the kinds of contact that might be made. It is not to be expected that any school would involve itself with all of these at once, or that the links would necessarily be continuous; but no school which wishes to play its part in its community can afford to ignore this field, and in to-day's society it is hardly being fair to its pupils if it does not.

Such contact can be a two way traffic. Some schools take their responsibility seriously enough to give the older children at least some opportunity of community service. This may take various forms; sponsored walks for local or national charities, clean-up operations (which must be properly supervised) in local parks or beauty spots; visits to the old and lonely; inviting pensioners to school entertainments; service to schools or homes for handicapped children; these are all current examples from middle schools which both appeal to children as a worth-while undertaking and help to build up in them a sense of social responsibility.

The last development to mention is the *community school*. Though the base is more often a secondary or an upper school, there is at least one recently opened community school for which the base is a middle school, and more may come. What the term denotes is that the school is part of a complex offering activities, and facilities are offered on the site to the whole community, adults as well as children. In addition to the school itself, there may also be such things as a public library, a health centre, a drama hall, a swimming pool, a sports hall, offices for public advisory services, and additional facilities for adult education. By mutual arrangement groups of children from the school benefit from using appropriate resources when they are not required for adult use—and frequently during school hours the sporting facilities and the drama hall will be free. In exchange, of course, school facilities useful to youth or adult groups will be available to them during the evenings and week-ends, some for educational use and some for clubs and societies. The concept is one intended to bring the whole community together in its study and its recreation, or at least to give it a forum where this kind of interchange and contact with one's neighbours can take place. The experience of community schools, whatever kind of school is their base, will be watched with very great interest, for it could exercise a profound influence on our ideas of both community and education.